Outcome Running will take you on new adventures both in running and life. Practicable. Enjoyable. Uplifting.

Pat Falvey,
Explorer, Entrepreneur, Inspirational Speaker

Eoin has completed the hard yards himself and now in Outcome Running he shares his experience and wisdom gained along the way. It's a book that can help you reach and live in the Positive Zone like Eoin does today.

Frank Greally,
Editor, Irish Runner

'With Outcome Running Eoin Ryan has come up with a very innovative concept linking the two passions of his life, coaching and running. This is self-help on the move and Eoin's conversational and humorous style of writing make this concept easy to understand and to apply. This book is for anyone who is interested in getting fit and feeling good about themselves.

Adrian Mitchell,
Managing Director, Irish Lifecoach Institute

This book is dedicated to anyone who wishes to bring more positivity to their lives. May your healthy mind and body take you closer to understanding your life's purpose. It is a journey to be enjoyed. Treasured. Use this book to set you on track or reaffirm your mission. Run wild. Run free.

To my wife Beata and our daughter Ella. Thank you both for coming into my life and filling it with love and happiness.

Average 2 Awesome

I've been hanging in the background.

Watching from my safe place.

Observing everyone else succeed,

Feeling some disgrace.

My abilities are equal,

My skill levels are high.

If only I would use them...

Then I'd do more than just get by.

Now I feel motivated

Driven by my goal.

I will no longer play second best,

And that excites my soul.

I wonder why I hesitated,

I wonder why I crawled,

The world is opening up for me;

My life has truly evolved!

Eoin Ryan
– Peak Performance Coach

Contents

Introduction   9

The Milestones   13

The First Milestone – Fun   17

The Second Milestone – Passion   31

The Third Milestone – Gratitude   41

The Fourth Milestone – Feedback   57

The Fifth Milestone – Significance   73

The Sixth Milestone– Generosity   85

The Seventh Milestone –Law of Attraction   97

The Eighth Milestone– Challenge   115

The Ninth Milestone–Flexibility   127

The Tenth Milestone– Strength   137

Goal Setting on Your Marks   151

Get Set for Flow   163

Goal Setting Go   173

Eoin's Story

Eoin Ryan is an entrepreneur, an award-winning peak performance coach, speaker and multiple road race organiser. But first and foremost he is a runner.

He has completed dozens of marathons, triathlons and Ironman races. In 2014, he finished one of the toughest races in the world: the Marathon des Sables – a 250km run through the punishing terrain and blistering heat of the Sahara Desert. Before that, he organised and completed a static Ironman in Grafton Street, Dublin – raising €40,000 for charity in a single day. He also ran seven marathons in six days along the canals of Ireland to raise money for Crumlin Children's Hospital.

Outcome Running is the new and improved version of Outcomerun, which was an Amazon Kindle No. 1 bestseller. It brings together all he has learned from running and from life itself, and explores his unique vision of the transformative power of running and positivity.

Introduction

This is a book for everyone. It's for those who've been running all their lives and those who want to start running. I'm not going to teach you how to run ultra-marathons or break records or win every time. What I will do is show you how you can harness the power of positivity to improve your running and your life.

I've been either playing sport or running my whole life – well, almost my whole life. I hit a slump in my mid-thirties and for a while took very little exercise. Without really planning to, I become a workaholic. My anxiety levels soared and my confidence levels slumped. When I was a younger man, I used to vent my stress through sport, but because I was inactive, there was nowhere for that stress to go. As a result, I became a very negative person.

Rediscovering my running mojo broke the cycle of negativity. The impact on my life was immediate. The cloud under which I had been living began to lift, my positivity returned, and allowed me to make all sorts of changes that I could never have initiated without the positivity that running unleashed. And ever since, I've seen countless numbers of my coaching clients kick-start the same transformation.

This book will take you through my unique system, which is laid out here in the form of a 10 mile (10Km) run – with each mile forming a staging point on the way to a faster, more positive you.

Running I believe is a great metaphor for life, and sometimes much more than a metaphor. I've noticed too that among the runners in my client list, there are always parallels between how they run and how they manage their lives.

I remember one woman who came to me burned out by the dating circuit. She told me she'd been trying to meet someone for years but despite her efforts had yet to meet 'the one'.

I knew she was a runner, so I asked her about that. When did she run? How did she run? Where did she run? She told me she had a circuit that she ran near her home. She did it at the same time in the same way every two days. It never varied. She never tried anything new. I asked her if she'd tried mountain running or beach running, if she ever thought about joining a running club or running with someone.

She hadn't. It was always the same old loop, over and over again. She remained firmly in her comfort zone and had decided that nothing of interest lay beyond it. She was unwilling to experiment, unwilling to expand.

I knew of a great coastal trail not far from where she lived. I suggested that she go there, to try it out, to think of it as a mini-adventure. Reluctantly, she agreed to give it a go. And of course she loved it. Making that little change was like tipping over the first domino. She fell back in love with running. It had become a chore, a necessary evil, just something she did to keep her weight down. Now it became fun (something we'll be talking about in more detail very soon). Plus, it gave her the impetus to open up to all kinds of new experiences, which ultimately put her on the path to a great new relationship.

The simple truth is that if you can create changes in your hobby, you can create all sorts of other changes in your life. Changes made through your running can be a soft touch in building confidence for the bigger decisions you need to make. Running allows you to expand your boundaries, discover new places and test yourself.

For years I've been encouraging my coaching clients to take up exercise. Why? Exercise put simply makes you feel good. And when we are enjoying ourselves, we are more open to learning and absorbing information. Walking, jogging or running are the easiest and most accessible introductions to exercise. This book is about how all the benefits of running can be spread throughout your life.

Life leaves clues about how we function. Can you see how the way you exercise (or don't exercise) is reflected in your everyday life? Are you half committed? Do you have lapses? Are you overtraining? Are you not running/exercising at all and feeling low? Think about it for a moment. Think about it honestly

Positivity

The idea for *Outcome Running* was sparked by a moment in a race. I was hurting, I was in pain, I didn't think I could continue. Then a spectator on the course hailed me with a smile and a high five. That –a little piece of human generosity and positivity – was all I needed to get me through the slump and drive me on to the finish line.

You will see positivity everywhere when you run. Fellow runners tend to say 'hi' when they meet you on the road. If you take part in road races, you'll come across people who have come out to cheer you on. A small clap, a cheer, a high five or a jellybaby can give you such a boost that for a few hundred metres you forget that you are tired or hurting.

What if you could replicate this feeling along the whole race course and eliminate all of your negative thoughts? Wouldn't that make things easier? Do you think it might help you to go faster?

This feeling can also be replicated in your everyday life. Wouldn't it be great if you could create those positive feelings every day?

Positivity is an amazing asset. It can enhance relationships, working lives and health. It relieves depression, it helps develop lives and broadens minds. In my opinion, positivity is more important than happiness because a positive mind can cope with both happiness and unhappiness. Positivity delivers resilience. A positive attitude will give you the resolve to bounce back more quickly from setbacks.

Positivity as a feeling is neither downloadable nor tradable. You can't acquire positivity – you have to open yourself to it and feel it. It lives within your head and heart space – concepts I'll discuss in more detail very soon. *Outcome Running* is a tool to help you develop and strengthen your levels of positivity through running.

Running

Running is at the core of so many sports: football, boxing and the three-legged race, to name but a few. It is also a sport that costs very little to start. Get yourself a proper pair of runners, shorts and running socks and you can call yourself a runner. It's much cheaper than horse riding, where a horse, at the very least, is mandatory. Plus, the road, the paths, the forests, mountains and parks are all out there ready for you.

Running for some is more than a hobby or pastime. It is a lifestyle. For those veteran runners, it often happens that it slips from enjoyment to routine to indifference. It has blended so deeply into your life that you feel compelled to go for a run. If you have lost your running mojo and feel that you have peaked, Outcome Running will reinvigorate your 'why' to go running.

However, Outcome Running is not a book solely about running. It's much more than that. The skills that allow you to improve your running can also be applied to your everyday life.

The Milestones

This book is based on ten milestones:

1	Fun	**6**	Generosity
2	Passion	**7**	The Law of Attraction
3	Gratitude	**8**	Challenge
4	Feedback	**9**	Flexibility
5	Significance	**10**	Strength

Taken together, these ten elements build to create a template for a more positive, faster you. The final section of the book takes you through a masterclass goal-setting programme, which will show you how to blend all that you have learned to allow you to achieve your best. I have used this strategy with hundreds of my peak performance coaching clients and regularly facilitate master classes for groups and corporate clients. I have researched and improved these strategies over time, adding tools that you won't find anywhere else.

It only takes a small trickle of water to start a new river. Once you start absorbing the ten milestones into your running and everyday life – consciously and subconsciously – the changes will begin to take root.

It will start as a trickle. My role in this partnership with you is to be your guide on this journey using my skills and experience.

In my coaching one-to-one sessions, clients have all the answers. I am only the means of helping them to unlock the truths they hold within them. So in the book, I will be refraining from giving advice because I can only base my advice on my own experiences. I can't speak on behalf of the world. I will throw in examples to stimulate thought. I'll talk about some clients and how they managed to turn their lives around through this system. You'll hear, too, about my own experiences – nearly becoming shark food on a trawler in the Torres Strait, and the business disaster that nearly ruined me but led ultimately to success.

Head Space and Heart Space

These concepts are central to my system. Most of us are lost in our heads, constantly thinking, analysing, judging, worrying and so on. That clutter can often block important messages coming from other areas of our bodies. It can often prevent you from connecting with your whole self, which is the term I use to describe someone engaging both head space and heart space. How can you hear what your gut and heart are telling you if there's too much noise in your head for those other voices to be heard?

We all need to pay more attention to our 'gut feelings'. We need to listen to our hearts to know when we are in conflict with our values. These organs are there to protect us and help keep us alive, so when they 'speak', they have something important to say.

Head Space

Head space is the domain of the ego. The ego will never allow you to be enough as you are. As far as it is concerned, you are lacking. Lacking money, lacking talent, lacking beauty, etc. The ego looks externally – to the world – to provide a solution or compensation for your perceived shortcomings.

But the world is not stable. Trends change, wars happen, technologies advance. So if you are constantly in your head (in a state of lacking) in this fast-changing world, you are constantly trying to keep up. The goalposts are always moving, so you will never win. Don't get me wrong. Head space can be on our side too. It is completely in favour of pursuing happiness and greater positivity. But this is where head space can get clouded.

'When I get this done, I'll be happy.'

'When I qualify, I'll be happy'.

'When the puppy stops eating my shoes, I'll be happy.'

Why are we pursuing happiness when it is already within us? We are conditioned to believe that happiness and other traits need to be pursued or earned. That is total 'head space' thinking. To be your whole self, a place where nothing is missing and you are at peace, you need to engage head and heart space.

Heart Space

Heart space is awareness of your whole self. Therefore, it is not opposite to head space, but rather complements it. When you are truly happy and aware, you are being your whole self. You lead from the heart,

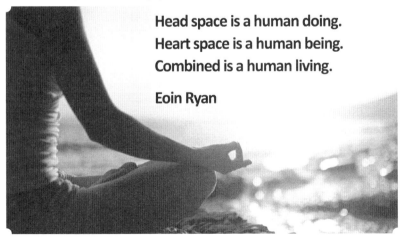

**Head space is a human doing.
Heart space is a human being.
Combined is a human living.**

Eoin Ryan

not from the head. There are no 'airs and graces' and no possessions needed to prop you up. You are just happy in your own skin.

So how can we open up a new level of consciousness to engage both the heart and the head be our whole self?

The first step lies in becoming aware of your feelings, acknowledging them and being able to detach yourself from them so you don't become a prisoner of any one experience. Take time to meditate and to think. Be kinder to yourself and others. Spend time in nature. Forgive yourself and others. Give thanks. Accept yourself.

I cover much of this material in the book. Plus, I also directly reference head and heart space through various examples. Engaging the ten milestones while you run will create a platform for you to get out of your head space and connect more with your heart space.

How to Use This Book

While each milestone is self-contained, all are interconnected. Before you go running, read and absorb a milestone. Think about the material as you run. Changing and enhancing your outlook on running *while* you are running can simultaneously change your outlook on life. This shows you that you are flexible and capable of change. Those feelings of success and positivity are transferable.

You'll find written exercises designed to help open up your thinking during each milestone, plus a brief review and action steps, which will prompt you to find ways of implementing the material in your life.

I also include running and race tips after each milestone, designed to help you to make the most of your running. And for more seasoned runners there are methodologies and tips to help you achieve better times. I'll show you how harnessing positivity can make a substantial difference to how you perform.

A fantastic journey lies ahead of you.

The First Milestone – Fun

One question I often ask my clients in my coaching sessions: What do you do for fun?

It's a simple question but it trips people up. They go blank. They smile awkwardly and stare at the ground as if they're trying to remember what the word means. They're thinking too hard about something that should be on the tip of the tongue. But it isn't. The logical left brain doesn't quite know how to handle it. The answer lies in the right brain, but we often don't know how to access it.

Western culture has become very left-brain focused. The left hemisphere of our brain functions as the logical, detail-orientated and strategic side, while the right hemisphere is in charge of our imagination, fun, memory, intuition and all our creative functions. We absorb with the left side of the brain and create with our right side.

Left brain
Reality based
Words and language
Detail orientated
Forms strategies
Focus on knowledge
Uses logic
Present and past
Practical
Maths and science
Focus on facts
Knows object name
Safe

Right brain

Symbols and images
Big picture orientated
Presents possibilities
Focus on beliefs
Uses feeling
Present and future
Spontaneous
Philosophy and religion
Focus on imagination
Knows object function
Risk-taking

Fun is a right-brain function often ignored or overlooked due to left-brain dominance. A lot of that is a legacy of the educational systems of which many of us are a product (though much has improved in that area in recent years). We just need to 'let our hair down' more and engage in more fun activities.

So what do you do for fun? After a lengthy pause, my clients will usually pick the old reliables like going to the cinema, eating out and concerts. But the length of the pause generally reflects how long it's been since they did any of these things.

You Are Designed to Run

Running was never meant to be fun; not at the beginning. In prehistoric times, it was the difference between eating and dying. Our early ancestors were hunter-gatherers and what better motivation could you possibly need to go running than as a means to feed yourself and your family?

Back then, 'persistence hunting' – running across vast distances in order to drive an animal to exhaustion – was paramount to survival, no matter what age you were. Everyone, young and old, took part, and if you didn't keep up, you didn't eat. In the absence of any physical weapons, tracking and pursuing an animal using distance running was

man's only weapon. Running a large herbivore to exhaustion took a lot of teamwork and persistence.

There is a tribe called the Tarahumara in Mexico which still maintains this level of endurance running. But for most people today, running is no longer about survival. Supermarkets are there to feed us 24/7. A blessing – or curse – of modern living is the effortless availability of on-demand convenience. We have swung from survival to overindulgence. In the context of a global obesity epidemic, perhaps our longevity once again depends on running and exercise in general! So if you are starting to run, bear in mind that running is what you are designed to do. You are – or will be – naturally brilliant at it!

My Kinda Fun

Not getting enough of your 'kinda fun' leads to frustration and boredom. And maybe even resentment. Fun is crucial to our being. If you believe you stopped playing with toys after your shoe size matched your age, take your smartphone out of your pocket and think again! Go to a child's playroom and stop yourself picking something up. Or open a big household catalogue book and try skipping over the toys section. I dare you! We never really lose our fun streak, we just suppress it.

Advertisers know this and try to appeal to our fun side with humorous ads to get our attention. But like humour, fun is subjective. When I was a child, we went to the National Botanic Gardens in Dublin once a year as a family because it was my father's idea of fun. He was having so much 'fun' that he read the name of every single plant in the whole of the gardens. The rest of the family prayed for rain!

Your kind of fun is very important to you because you are important. You have freedom of choice to create any kind of fun you like and enjoy it. Often, however, other people have to be taken into account (I hope my father reads this!). There will, naturally enough, be times when you may have to 'fall in' and be a team player; although sometimes it might be better to decline than go under duress. Unless you are a brilliant actor, your demeanour will give you away.

According to the eminent psychologist Albert Mehrabian, most of our communication is non-verbal. Words account for 7 per cent, tone of voice accounts for 38 per cent, and body language for 55 per cent. (I must point out that those percentages apply to the communication of feelings and attitudes. For example: you might say you are happy but the tone of your voice and your folded arms tell a different story.) What this means is you'll do very well to hide your true feelings from others. People pick up on this and then you are in danger of ruining someone else's fun. I trust your judgment to make the right decision. Be mindful, you always have choices.

First Milestone Questionnaire

I want you to do the following exercises on fun. Think about it and be honest. Remember that if you don't know where you are, how can you expect to know where you are going? Please do this now

Note: I've included running as one of your five in Stage 2. This can be replaced with walking or jogging, whichever best describes your fitness aspirations. To realise the best possible improvements in your life via Outcome Running, it is important that you bring running or walking into your routine.

FUN

Stage 1

Define what fun means to you. _____

_____

Stage 2

Put a tick to the side of zero that most represents your present situation.

Having my kind of fun ——————— Having other people's fun

+1   0   -1

Both

Populate the five boxes with examples, but at least **3 of the 5** should be with your kind of fun.

Running (get you started)				

Outcome question: What do you need to change to have more of your kind of fun?

_____

_____

Meet Your Inner Child

Your 'inner child' is always with you. But as adults, with expectations of certain behaviours, we tend to detach ourselves from our inner child. The inner child has no voice, so it is often forgotten or neglected. It is ignored – and when you ignore a child, what generally happens? It cries. It cries out for attention, it cries out for your attention. It wants to play, to be nurtured. To have fun.

Your inner child never leaves you. It will always be with you until the day you die – as will your inner adult. And depending on what age you are in life, you could already be the 'inner grandparent'. That is the third phase of your life. If that is the case, you have the wisdom of all three, if, of course, you choose to acknowledge them.

Connect with Your Inner Child

Put down this book and sit up straight, feet on the floor and arms on your lap. Close your eyes and imagine yourself looking at your inner child. Now think about what you wrote in the outcome question on fun. Ask your inner child if this is what they want? If you were very playful as a child, they might want that – more playfulness. Stay with your inner child and when ready to leave, thank them for their participation. Agree that you will visit again. Open your eyes.

Some children are shy and slower to reveal what they truly feel. If you were like that as a child, it may take you a few attempts to reconnect. I didn't have much interaction with children for most of my life. It just happened that way. That changed when my sister had three kids. One of them said to me one day 'You're very bossy'. Wow! That was direct feedback. He was 100 per cent correct too; I was being very bossy. I was failing to connect with him, because I was struggling to build a bridge between my inner adult and inner child. I needed to try harder or simply practise connecting more with my inner child.

Trying to reconnect with your inner child is likely to be an emotional experience. But your new friend may be a gateway to rekindling your fun side. Your outward expression of your inner child is to have fun. Children can make fun out of any situation; everything is fun! How much easier would it be to see life and its challenges as fun? Remember that you still have your inner adult as a supervisor; it will rein you in.

Not having much of 'my kinda fun'? Engage your inner child to help make life more fun. I was oblivious to my inner child; he was always there, but I never acknowledged him. I was disconnected. Hence, the 'bossy' tag I was deservedly given by my nephew. For most of my twenties, fun was associated with drinking alcohol. It became my crutch. I lost my natural fun side. I took life outside drinking very seriously. The realisation that I had an inner child came only after I had blocked out every bit of fun (including drinking) to become a workaholic.

For the first three years of setting up my sports events business as a race organiser, I put in unforgiving hours at a desk. I hardly ran and lost contact with my friends. My bank balance was my report card. I knew it was wrong but I had no companion to listen to me and guide me. I was completely stuck and felt trapped in this routine. My left brain was telling me to keep going. However, a faint voice in the background was trying to communicate with me. That voice I discovered was my inner child. He gets my attention now. I welcome him, and his demands for fun. I encourage you to pay attention to your inner child and consider making him your totem for fun. My experience is only one example; your rekindled friendship with your inner child could be even better.

Running and My Inner Child

I bring my inner child running with me all the time. Running in new places can be just like having a new adventure. You see new things, meet new people and can enjoy the fullness of nature in its seasons. How many times have I said to myself, 'I never thought I'd be running here'. You can run over mountains, through parks (not safari parks) and on streets in cities. The variety provides much of the fun. And it works just like that with life in general. The more variety you can pack into your life, the greater the fun you will have. Aim to do something new and different at least once a week. The best fun is very often free.

And so is running. Be creative with your running and go to different places. Engage the right side of your brain and think of all the new, fun places you could run. When I run, I tend not to do the same things over again. I like to be adventurous, to explore, to check things out, like a child who has learned to walk. I like to get lost. I'll run into a housing estate and see if there's a way out the back. Yes, I may end up having to backtrack, but if I do manage to find a way through, the experience becomes that little bit richer.

Okay, sometimes, if I'm aiming for a particular challenge and I'm on a strict training programme, I have to grade, plan and time the run carefully, but if I'm between targets, I take off my running watch and just see where my feet bring me. Maybe I'll decide that I'm only taking left turns today, or I'll find another runner and strike up a conversation with him or her.

> *Twenty years from now you will be more disappointed by the things that you didn't do than by the ones you did do. So throw off the bowlines. Sail away from the safe harbour. Catch the trade winds in your sails. Explore. Dream. Discover.*
>
> Mark Twain

My Fun Catalyst

Quotes can be life-changing. I can remember the day I first read the quote above from Mark Twain. It was the first quote to make me stop in my tracks and think. It was the inspiration I needed at the right time, almost as if he had written it for me. For me, it was a permission slip to have more fun. If I kept working, working, working, I was going to stay in a very safe, sheltered and dreary harbour. So I got up, got out and started running again. I never looked back.

Outcome Running: Getting Your Thoughts in Order

The next time someone asks you what do you do for fun, tell them you're a runner (or walker). Never be stuck for an answer. It doesn't matter what level you are at. Never apologise for being new, for being back-of-the-field or casual. Say it loud and proud. I am a runner.

Engage the right side of your brain and make fun happen for you. Reconnect with your inner child and see how he or she can help you to access your fun side. Invite them to come on a run with you. Imagine them there beside you, smiling and focused. Encourage them and support them. You are the beneficiary of this positive self-talk too. In the early stages of a run, you are fresh and invigorated. Smile and say hello to the people you pass, and to fellow runners. You'll almost always get a salute back. It's fleeting – but it's nice. It costs nothing and it shows that you are friendly and approachable.

Action Steps

1. Make a decision: 'I will have more fun in my life. And it's going to be mostly my kind of fun.'
2. If you're having trouble identifying your kind of fun, try to connect with your inner child. See what she or he has to say.
3. If you're very routine orientated, make a determined effort to change to routines that include more fun.

Running Tip

If you have been inactive for a long period or are new to running, I suggest a visit to your doctor, particularly if any of the following applies to you:

- You've been sedentary for a year or more.
- You don't currently exercise and are over age 65.
- You have been diagnosed with heart trouble.
- You're pregnant.
- You're overweight.
- You're a current or former smoker.
- You have high blood pressure.
- You have diabetes.
- You have a family history of heart disease.
- You have chest pain, especially when exerting yourself.
- You often feel faint or have severe dizzy spells.
- You have another medical condition.

Better to be safe than sorry.

Racing Tip

Over the ten years I've been organising races, I've seen quite a few avoidable mistakes made by participants, usually because they arrive at the race poorly informed. This year, I will organise nine separate races with a total participation of more than 12,000 people. That's a lot of people to manage, so having detailed race information available is really important.

If you're attending a race, always read that race information. It will make a huge difference to your enjoyment of the day if you know what's going on. And for any newbies, it will make your race day experience memorable for the right reasons. You may never return if you mistakenly start the marathon when you were only there for the fun 5K!

When I put together race information, I always work on the assumption that (a) this is someone's first race and (b) they have never been to this location before. Assuming the race information is available, print it off, read it and bring it with you. You'd be surprised at the amount of times I'm asked on race day 'What time is the race starting at?'.

The Second Milestone – Passion

Passion is a step further than excitement or enthusiasm. Passion is a drive that exudes dedication and constant momentum towards achieving a goal in your life. It is within all of us but some consider it 'lost' because they haven't engaged it.

For a period in my life I did consider my passion lost. I'd be surprised if I was alone on this one. I, like many others, was on a quest to find my passion. And after many near misses and 33 years, I finally found it. And guess what? It was right under my nose all the time. I simply wasn't reading the signals or joining the dots. Why? Simply because I didn't know how to do it. I'll recount my story. It might resonate with you.

How I Found My Passion

My journey in life was a classic Irish middle-class journey. Education was valued in our house, so going to college was always the target. The thing is, it wasn't my target. I had none. I had no idea what I wanted to do. I drifted. I took the path of least resistance. In college, I studied subjects that I was good at in school. In my last year in as an Arts student, aware that I was still in the doldrums, I started to try to make things happen. I applied for and got a role as the student representative for a beer company. This exposed me to blue chip company practices and marketing. A large part of the job was to support clubs and societies. Because of that job, I decided to do a one-year Higher Diploma in Marketing. From there, I spent 18 months travelling the world before I went looking for a real job.

I worked in marketing for seven years. Looking back now, I think it was obvious that I had only moderate passion for this line of work. Certainly, nothing like the level of passion I now give to my coaching clients or my road race business. The thing is – what I didn't realise – was that my real passion had always centred on helping people. I held my first charity fundraiser when I was eleven. I organised a Halloween disco for my class and raised £20 for an autism charity.

Years after that, I spent three months doing voluntary work in a home for abandoned and disabled kids in Argentina. When I got home, I ran two marathons for the same home, and held five table quizzes. I did a static Ironman race on Grafton Street, Dublin for People in Need in 2007. I ran seven marathons in six days for the National Children's Hospital in 2008. And when I was in-between jobs, I worked for the charity Saint John of God. In 2014, I completed the Marathon des Sables for the suicide charity, Pieta House. And in 2016, I organised the Patrick Pearse 5K run for the Argentine charity. I'm not relating all this to set myself up as some kind of saint. Helping people is just something that I love to do. I really come alive and feel passionate when I do something that I feel is making a difference. I am operating from heart space.

When I was in the throes of these challenges, especially the sporting ones, I couldn't fail. My mind and body were at one. If I became tired, if the negative voices crept into my mind, I recalled the faces of the children I'd worked with in Argentina. There was nothing better to refocus me. I was deep in the heart space zone.

Recounting all this, it's so obvious now that helping people should have formed a central part of what I chose to do with my life. Becoming self-employed gave me the freedom to qualify as a life coach, which in turn fulfilled my desire to help people. I believe that our passions are within us; often, right under our noses. It took me a long time to join the dots and finally notice mine. Passion is a feeling – it isn't something that is out there to be acquired; it is built into you. You exude it when you talk about or do something you are passionate about.

Think about what makes you passionate. Maybe you'll find it quicker than I did. Or maybe you'll have to journey a little further into life to notice the signals. I spent a lot of years working in jobs I didn't really have a passion for. But I don't consider that time wasted. I learned a great deal about marketing and selling, skills that continue to come in handy in the work I do today. If you can accept that you won't make all the correct decisions in life, it can make your past a lot more acceptable.

And while you can't change the past, you can change how you deal with it. Life is about experiences and adventure – trial and error. You will make mistakes; make sure you take the positive and learn from them.

When you lose, don't lose the lesson.

Anonymous

No Age Limit

Do you remember when you were a child? The stages of curiosity began with putting everything into your mouth to taste it, followed by walking around to see and touch more things. We began to talk, we began to explore our world. To a child, everything is new and everything is interesting. Much of what we learned in our early development moulded us. One thing we all have in common as bigger people, besides being potty-trained, is that our levels of curiosity have flat lined. Ask yourself, when was the last time you did something new?

It seems the older we get, the more we settle into routines and ruts. We do the same things day in and day out and we wonder why we are bored! Where's the passion in that? The sad truth is that many have resigned themselves to this way of existing. Then they do nothing about it, except complain or focus their energies on the salvation of the weekend. So let's narrow the question to: When was the last time you did something new at the weekend? Think about it. I bet your weekend has its measure of standard routines.

I know that we all have responsibilities, and we can't just throw them up and go off on an adventure, but that doesn't mean we can't find time in our lives to engage our passions.

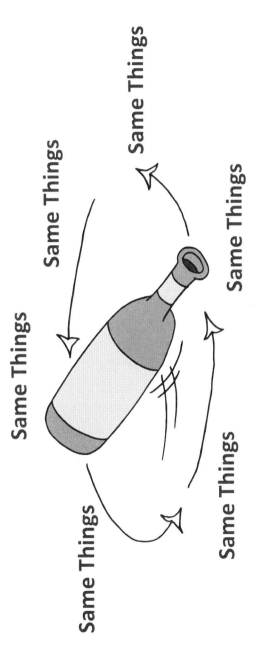

How to Take Ownership of Your Passions

Everyday responsibilities might be paramount, but unless **you** decide to change things, nothing will change. The big question is how. How do you bring more passion into your life? Firstly, look at the clues life gives you. Look back at a time when you felt you were living a fuller life. What were you doing? What was inspiring you at that time? Take some quiet time and look back over all the things you enjoy doing, past and present.

Think about the things that you always yearned to do but never did. Is the flame still burning? If it is, then get up and do it. Yes, we all have responsibilities and jobs that *must* be done, but most of us have untapped passions we're just not getting around to. It's the easiest thing in the world to find reasons not to do something. The truth is that there will never be a perfect time to try, so why not now! Look around and see what interests you. Look around and see what annoys you! What repels you? What draws you? Either can fire your passion. Do you feel something lighting you up? Nurture it and give it a go. Bring back your innate childhood curiosity. Bring back your sense of adventure. If you are already a runner, take a trip to a new park or hillside. Give that familiar loop or the 'out and back' run you usually do a break. Our passion is like a fire – it needs to be kindled and stoked.

Have a go at the following exercises. Stage 2 and the outcome question are flexible, and can be past or present. Work from the present back.

PASSION

Stage 1

Are you excited about your life and turned on by the things you do **daily**?
On a scale of 1 to 10 (10 being excellent), circle: 1   2   3   4   5   6   7   8   9   10

Stage 2

What are the three main things that you were/are passionate about?

A. _____

B. _____

C. _____

On a scale of 1 to 5 (5 being highest level) grade your levels of passion in the grey box opposite each.

Outcome question: Write down how you felt/feel while doing A, B & C?

1) Can this feeling of passion be transferred to areas of your **daily** life?
2) Can a **new** passion with the same feelings be integrated into your **daily** life?

_____

_____

_____

What, No Passion?

Here is a profoundly unscientific test from the institute of my intuition. I believe that if you are really passionate about something, you will dream about it. Works for some, won't work for all. My theory is that if you are passionate about something, it will be processed in your subconscious mind while you sleep. For example, a few days before a race I am organising, I will always have a nightmare that I've forgotten to organise some crucial component that messes up the race. It wakes me up every time in a panic! It sucks, but I'm used to it. I'm passionate about putting on a great race. Trust me –there is something in dreams hinting at passion.

Should you draw a blank on passion, then you are a blank canvas. Great! I suggest that you start running. Running is a hobby, unless you become very good at it! It is not weekend dependent. And workaholics with several children do it on a regular basis. It makes you feel good via the release of happy hormones and it is very sociable. It gets you out in nature and helps keep your weight in check. That's a lot of pros. I know a guy from school who was a heavy smoker and never got off his couch during his twenties. He took up running when he was 32. These days he's actually winning races. Running became his passion.

Outcome Running: Getting Your Thoughts in Order

Passion lies within us all. We can only have passion for something we are experiencing or have feelings for. Passion levels vary and what gets some people's passions stirring won't cut it for someone else. Find people with the same passions and interests as you and you could open up a whole new circle of friends. Maybe it will be in a running club or running group or even a relationship. Passion kicks in when you've a target time in mind for a training run or race. If your legs start to tire with a couple of miles or kilometres to go, passion helps to fuel that extra bit of effort. The same goes for the project that is your life. If you're not currently feeling any passion for anything in your life, use your hobby to get the fires burning again. Experiencing passion through your hobby gives you the know-how to cross-fertilise it into other parts of your life.

Action Steps

1. What made you passionate in the past? Look for the clues that probably lie all around you.
2. Still no passion? Take up running and try new things to freshen up your life. Life has plenty of experiences just waiting for you to discover. Be open-minded.
3. Aim to extend your passion beyond the confines of the weekend. Use the full seven days. Change your routine to make space for it.

Running Tip

Doctors say that runners make the worst patients. Why? Because we never wait until we are fully healed before we return to running. I'm certainly guilty of this. And I've seen this time and again with people who take up running after being sedentary for awhile. They take to running with a passion. As a result, they want to do more training and longer races than their bodies can cope with. Then injury strikes. Suddenly, all these great new sensations come to an abrupt stop, creating one unhappy runner. That can spoil the fun, mess up your new routine and stall your passion.

Don't fall prey to this. Think long term. There is no 'racing season'. You can race at any stage in the year. So build it up slowly. You don't have to enter every race on the calendar. Enjoy the journey. And if you find yourself injured – listen to the experts and allow enough healing time.

Racing Tip

There can sometimes be a temptation in races to go out too fast. Give it everything and then die a slow death to the finish line. Not a great idea! You should aim to spread your energies over the course of the race. Ideally, you should aim to complete the first half of a race at the same pace as the second half – known as neutral splits. Or better still, complete the second half faster – negative splits (rarely done however). So if you run a 10 mile/km race, the second half should take you as long (or quicker) than the first half, barring any major hills or winds on an out-and-back course.

While doing this, it is important to listen to your heart rate. If you have a calibrated heart rate monitor, it will quickly tell you if you are overdoing or under doing it. If you don't have one and are able to chit-chat comfortably during a race, then you are probably under pace (especially on the shorter 5K or 10K races). Remember if you are doing a long race, slow down the pace.

The Third Milestone – Gratitude

I once worked on a prawn trawler, fishing the waters between Australia and Papua New Guinea. An unlikely place for a backpacker to end up, but that was exactly why I chose to be there. I wanted adventure. I got what I wanted, but the whole thing very nearly ended in tragedy. It was about two weeks into the trip and we were all working away at what they called 'the table', sorting through the catch. We worked at night, when the prawn were out, and slept during the day. It was a rough night – not quite stormy but there was a heavy swell–and the stool at which I worked wasn't quite right. One leg was shorter than the others, which meant that in addition to the rocking of the boat, I also had to manage the rocking of the stool. Any time I felt a big wave coming, I had to wedge my elbows in tight to the sides of the table – which was basically a big tray – just to keep from being tossed overboard.

Sorting the catch sounds fairly simple. It was anything but! We may have been fishing for prawns, but those nets pulled up all sorts of sea creatures. Crazy looking things, the like of which I'd never seen before or since. There were sharks, sea snakes, manta rays and electric eels. I'd even heard of some boats pulling up saltwater crocodiles. The thing was, we had to sort all these things by hand. And we couldn't wear gloves, because not alone did you have to sort the prawn from all the things that weren't prawn, you also had to categorise the prawns by size. Gloves would have made that job too slow.

Around the Great Barrier Reef, every single thing you pull out of the sea is armed to the teeth with all kinds of natural defences. If it doesn't have teeth, it has spines; if it doesn't have spines, it has claws, or it can give you an electric shock or poison you! And your job is to dip your hands into this wriggling mass of live, hostile seafood. The first week, between poison and bites and so on, my hands swelled to one and a half times their normal size. Plus, you can't take your time over this. You work fast while you're fishing, to make the most of the hours of darkness. The large nets are hauled up four times throughout the night. You've got to empty the table of the first net's catch before the next comes, and it takes great concentration and dexterity to get everything done, grab a quick breather and start all over again.

Anyway, we're working away at our positions when I hear a creaking noise, a snap and hear a cable go whistling past my ear. I froze.

'Get down!' someone shouted.

I dropped. Next thing the boom – the huge metal post that extended out over the water – swung inwards, stopping just where my head had been moments before. The skipper had no choice at that moment but to cut the fishing equipment from the boom, which he did, and rapidly (placing a marker on the GPS so he could retrieve it later). But as soon as that heavy burden was cut away, the boat lurched over onto its other side. We suddenly took on a load of water, the engine room flooded, killing the power and leaving the boat stuck there at a 50 degree angle.

The skipper burst into action to save the fishing gear, the boat and then the crew. (I'm pretty sure I have that in the right order!) To do this, he took a serious risk. He set out to salvage the rest of the fishing gear, which was suspended from the other boom (still intact) and extended out over the water at a 90 degree angle to the boat. Long story short, his efforts backfired, making things suddenly worse. When he realised his error, he reacted quickly and put his life on the line to save both us and the boat. He grabbed a hacksaw and climbed out onto the 10-metre boom, which was rocking heavily, frequently submerging itself in the swell. Drowning was not his first concern, however. He wouldn't be afforded that luxury.

Each night, the boat was followed by either sharks or dolphins. It was never both. The order seemed to be dictated by whichever of these got there first. That night, it was sharks. I'd often watched the feeding frenzy when all of those things that were not prawn went sliding down the 'shit shoot' from the table into the water. It was a compelling sight, particularly for a guy who'd never quite gotten over the fear that the film *Jaws* had left in him. We watched the skipper from a higher point of the boat, one that wasn't being continually submerged. With one arm wrapped about the boom, he was trying to cut the cable with the hacksaw. But it just wasn't working. He needed both hands in order to apply sufficient force.

My survival instincts kicked in and I was halfway up the mast to climb out onto the boom when he eventually called for help. The problem – one of the problems – was that my added weight on the outstretched boom pulled the boat even lower into the waves. What we were about to do had to work. In poker terms, we were all in. I had to time my moves very carefully as I inched my way out, so that I could be static and clinging tight when each wave hit – otherwise I'd be gone. The last few metres, as the boom trailed into the water, were particularly hairy, but I made it. Once there, he didn't need to give me any instructions; I knew what to do. I lay on top of him, pinning him to the boom so he could cut the cable with both hands.

Every time the waves submerged us we were vulnerable to shark attack. All it took was one curious bite and both of us would be dead meat. Holding both our weights on this heaving, shifting boom took all my strength. I couldn't swim at the time and wasn't very good at coordinating breaths. We were constantly being dunked into the water. Each time we went under, I waited, teeth gritted for the first bite. Time goes very slowly when you are in a life-or-death situation. It seemed to take him forever to cut the cable. When he finally got through it and the heavy fishing gear fell into the sea, the boom sprung upwards. We were now just above the water – great – but the next challenge was to try and crawl backwards on this six-inch-wide, wet and slippery steel boom. This was actually the worst part.

Now that we were above the water, I could see them clearly. The sharks. Just like in the film, I could see the dorsal fins – which were a ghostly grey in the darkness – scudding through the churning water beneath us. Getting back would have been difficult on a calm day. But it was dark and the water was heaving and rolling beneath us. I remember edging backwards, on all fours, with the skipper barking at me to hurry up, until I got to the centre of the boom. At that point, I had to try to turn around, get up and walk back the rest of the way. One slip meant certain death. I will never forget touching down on the deck of that boat. I will never forget being overcome with the feeling of gratitude. There was hardly a part of my body that didn't hurt; I was stuck on a half-sunken trawler in the middle of the Torres Strait, but I was overcome with a feeling of pure gratitude. Gratitude for simply being alive.

Thankfully, it didn't come to this

The Power of Gratitude

So what has all that got to do with running or positivity? Simply this: gratitude is an exceptionally powerful force. By simply adopting an attitude of gratitude, you are welcoming this force into your life. And once there, it is capable of unleashing all kinds of positive dividends.

There's an old saying I firmly believe to be true: 'If you've forgotten the language of gratitude, you'll never be on speaking terms with happiness.'

There is a direct link between gratitude and happiness. I'm not talking here about simply remembering your Ps and Qs – although there is of course a connection. So much of our communication these days has been chopped and shortened. Emails, texts and instant messages have reduced please and thanks to *pls* and *thx*. Are we reaching a point where these words might disappear altogether? Simply because they're too much hassle to type? Gratitude is in danger of being shrugged off by society simply because it's too cumbersome and time consuming to bother with.

> *As we express our gratitude, we must never*
> *forget that the highest appreciation is not to utter words,*
> *but to live by them.*
>
> John F. Kennedy

Gratitude, however, is not just a question of good manners. Studies have demonstrated that depression is inversely correlated to gratitude. The more grateful a person is, the less depressed they are. Philip Watkins, a clinical psychologist at Eastern Washington University, found that clinically depressed individuals showed significantly lower gratitude levels (nearly 50 percent less) than non-depressed controls.

When my clients come to see me, we often take a look at their gratitude levels. It's very common for them to be unaware of gratitude or how powerful it can be. Gratitude has lost significance because we tend to focus more on what we don't have rather than what we do. That's a product of the society we live in. Marketing and advertising are constantly trying to catch our attention and create desire for an endless stream of products and gizmos. I worked in marketing for seven years and I vied for your attention with the best of them. But all of that conspires to leave us feeling inadequate if we don't have the latest, most up-to-date things. And that in turn distracts us from seeing what we *do* have.

The truth, however, is that most of us are surrounded by abundance; we have access to shelter, few will go hungry and we live in relative safety. But we don't tend to be grateful for this. Instead, we cultivate notions of scarcity. The glass always appears half-empty. The focus is upon the material things we lack or on someone who's better at doing something than we are. Bottom line – we see what we don't have and we believe that we are hard done by as a result. This is not a fruitful existence and can lead people down a path of depression and resentment.

A Higher Level of Being

Gratitude is about far more than just manners or gestures. Gratitude is a portal to a deeper connection with the universe. The positive energy exchanged when gratitude is created and accepted delivers a flow of harmony between two people. It is a dance between living beings, both operating from their heart space. The flow from heart space has no boundaries and can radiate from you to the four corners of the universe. It is beyond measure. It exists in limitless quantities, but many people choose to limit their supply to the universe, thus reducing their own contentment.

Think of a ray of light pulsating from your heart each time you demonstrate gratitude. Close your eyes and imagine what this looks like. Feel the sensation of the light all around you. Close your eyes again, but this time put your hand over your heart and try to stop that same radiant light illuminating you and the people around you. How did you feel when you purposefully shielded this beautiful light from yourself and others? I bet it didn't feel right to cover up something so radiant and natural. It was effortless to share the light but it took an effort to hide it from view. Our natural and harmonious flow of energy involves extending the light from our hearts, in many forms of expression, including gratitude.

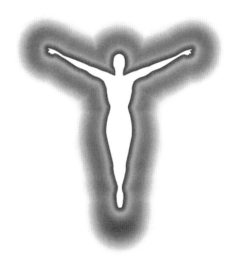

Make a decision to allow the light from your heart to shine all the time without eclipse or shadow. It may not always be reciprocated but as long as you give, you are open to the possibility of receiving. If you want gratitude in your life, give gratitude to other people. You need not concern yourself with conserving it. There is abundance. The secret of reaching contentment is to realise and accept that you have abundance in your life. When you adopt this shift of thinking into your daily life, you can give light – unconditionally – in the form of gratitude. You can become a master at this. It will be a subtle shift for some and a meteoric shift for others. The journey starts today.

You only get what you give.   New Radicals

Karina's Smile

I once spent three months volunteering in a home for abandoned and disabled kids in Argentina. Again, it was a quest for adventure, a response to my passions. The journey in was gruelling. I flew into Buenos Aires and caught an overnight bus to a place called Oberá, where I was picked up by the priest who was running the centre. We arrived there in the dead of night; he showed me to my bare little room then left for his own house. I was utterly exhausted from nearly forty hours of travel, but that first night, I'll never forget the cries and occasional screams that echoed through the building. And the next morning, I awoke out of a shallow doze to a chorus of cries and screams. The heat was intense. I was parched.

I got dressed and emerged warily from my room, walking up past rows of beds that I hadn't seen in the darkness the night before, past children with the most profound mental and physical disabilities. For a while I was lost among them. In the heat and with that sickly hospital smell lying thick about everything, I couldn't find the kitchen or the staff room. I was utterly disorientated and, if I'm honest, quite scared. I'd spent three months diligently learning Spanish, but when I eventually found the other workers I couldn't make myself understood at all. It turned out that the Spanish I had been learning on Linguaphone was an entirely different dialect to the one spoken in South America, and though there were similarities, my halting interpretation and lousy pronunciation made communication very difficult.

That morning, still half dead from the journey, I was overcome with doubt. My biggest fear was that I'd end up just a useless wallflower, that I wouldn't be accepted by either the workers or the patients, and that I'd never play a constructive role. But this is what happened. When I left the kitchen and came into the common area, a little girl came up to me. Karina, I would find out, was always the first to approach strangers. She walked up to me, took my hand and turning her face upwards, she smiled the most beautiful, crooked smile that I had ever seen. And at that moment, I thought, wow, I have a friend. This is going to work. Again, I was overcome with a sense of gratitude to her for the power of her welcome. And just as on the boat, it took a moment – where my comfort zone was far, far away – before I acquired the perspective to appreciate the splendour of being alive.

A Gratitude Journal

Very often we only appreciate what we have when it is taken away from us. Take health for example. Think of all the things you can do in the fullness of your health and then imagine losing the use of your legs. Imagine your gratitude at being able to walk or run again. Being able to walk again would become your sole focus, whereas before you may never have given it a thought. Think about someone you know who is recovering from mobility problems or ill-health. Is there another, similar scenario you can empathise with?

That example may only motivate you for a little while. But the truth is that we don't have to wait for a crisis to ignite lasting gratitude. Why not be grateful for everything you have here and now? To do this, I recommend to my clients that they keep a Gratitude Journal. Ask yourself: what are the five main things I am grateful for right now?

I am grateful for_____

I am grateful for_____

I am grateful for_____

I am grateful for_____

I am grateful for_____

Write them down in a journal specifically for this project. Then add to it every day. Very soon you will have pages of examples showing what you are grateful for. And as you run, think about all of the things that facilitate you:

I'm grateful for the paths I can run on.

I'm grateful for the clean air I have to breathe.

I'm grateful for the other runners who keep me company.

I'm grateful for the ability I have to run.

I'm grateful for the running shoes protecting my feet.

I'm grateful for the stretch in the evenings.

I'm grateful for the wildlife that I see when I run.

I'm grateful for the watch that tells me I'm going too slow or too fast.

I'm grateful for the people working at the water stations.

I'm grateful for the hill that tests my progress.

I'm grateful for the joy of being alive.

When I run, meditating on gratitude for everything that has brought me to this point delivers a very powerful high. Try it! Instead of allowing your brain to slip into a mindless state, catalogue all of the things that have given you the privilege of being able to run – because it is exactly that, a privilege. Feel the power of gratitude coursing through your veins. Running is just one aspect of your life to be grateful for. There are so many more. By bringing more gratitude into your life, you will start to achieve a higher level of being. Not only are you grateful for the small things, but you can stand back from the great moments in your life and appreciate those too.

Outcome Running: Getting Your Thoughts in Order

An attitude of gratitude will serve you well. Remember that those of us who can exercise are the lucky ones. There are so many who would love to be in your shoes. I often think of the kids in the home in Argentina when I'm out running. Most of them have since passed away. They never had an opportunity to experience walking – let alone going for a run. I often invite their spirits on runs with me so they can keep me company and experience it.

A race is a special place to be. Here you are, out in nature, with a bunch of strangers united in a common challenge. Brothers and sisters in sport if you like. Remember that they are a contributing part to your enjoyment of the atmosphere and experience. And even though you might like to beat them, they are enhancing your day, too. Thank them in your own private way. People who are injury-prone tend to be more grateful when it comes to being able to run. When something is taken away from us, we appreciate it more. So I'm advocating being grateful for everything in advance. Maybe that will soften your step and make your feet lighter on those training days and races.

GRATITUDE

Stage 1

Do you have an attitude of gratitude?   Yes / No

What can you do to improve your levels of gratitude and with whom?

_____

_____

Stage 2

How do you feel when someone neglects to show gratitude towards you?

_____

_____

Now that you are aware of your own feelings, you are responsible to extend gratitude towards others. Do you agree? Yes / No

Outcome question: How motivated are you to add to your gratitude diary?

On a scale of 1 to 10 (10 being excellent), circle   1   2   3   4   5   6   7   8   9   10

Action Steps

1. Let's make manners fashionable again. Become a good manners ambassador.
2. If you feel overly negative, keep a Gratitude Journal. Add to it regularly.
3. Is there someone in your life who once helped you, someone to whom you owe a debt of gratitude? Go visit them and thank them. Studies have shown that this little exercise can give your wellbeing a huge boost.

Running Tip

When you start running/exercising, there are a lot of training options open to you. Which one you pick will depend on how you identify yourself. Are you a newbie? A hobby jogger? A lapsed jogger? A fair-weather runner? A slogger? A club runner? Or just curious to see what all the fuss is about? Whatever you call yourself will probably determine your early aspirations when it comes to racing. Perhaps you have no ambitions to take part in a race. I believe that everyone should enter a race early on. It tends to provide the *Aha!* moment, when you'll understand why running is so popular, and why people keep training come rain or shine.

Learn from people who have already achieved what you want to do. Join a running group or a club. You can of course find a wealth of information, including training plans, online, but you wouldn't go see a doctor who qualified by only doing an online course and never attended a physical patient, would you?

Racing Tip

Never try anything new on race day. That goes for nutrition, gear or your warm-up routine. Race day is not the time for experimentation.

I can recall my first marathon in 2002. I never in my life saw so many people getting sick before a race. I thought what a nervous bunch they are. But it wasn't nerves, it was the sports gels they were using. People saw the sports gels for the first time in the Marathon Expo the day before and bought them to try them out. Many found them so sweet that they induced vomiting. In a matter of seconds, their nutritional plan for the morning was on the street in front of them. Not good. Instead, try new things on your training runs.

The same goes for new gear. Use your short runs to break in a new pair of runners. Otherwise, you are heading for blister territory. Lastly, if you see someone warming up and doing some gravity defying move, don't try to imitate. They might be a yoga instructor. Stick to what you know so you don't injure yourself before you get going.

The Fourth Milestone – Feedback

We're all happy to hear about what we've done well, but it's not quite so easy to hear about our weaknesses. It takes both honesty and guts to absorb feedback and work it into your life. One of the toughest arguments you will ever have with yourself is about admitting to failure. I had two clients, both of whom liked to run competitively. Both invested a lot of time and energy in getting faster. Both hired a running coach and trained hard. Within a month of each other, both came into my office having underperformed in races that they had big ambitions for. The first guy told me what went wrong.

'The day was so windy!' he said, 'and the race was way oversubscribed. They let too many people on the road, and I just couldn't get through.'

The more he talked, the angrier he became, remembering the experience of the race. Even the smallest negative details were recounted.

'Then at the water station, they gave me orange instead of water!'

As far as he was concerned, everything that went wrong had been outside of his control. As far as his underperformance went, he was blameless. My other client told me – without rancour – that her mistake was preventable.

'I started too far down the field. I should have placed myself near the front to avoid the slower runners. Next time, I've got to make sure that I'm nearer the front.'

See the difference? My first client had absolved himself of all blame for his performance and in so doing scuppered his chances of learning from the experience. My second client, however, saw ways to improve next time. Both failed, but only one saw failure as a feedback opportunity. Our minds are programmed to stay consistent with the story we believe. My first client will talk about the race and the more he repeats that story, the more fixed in his mind it will become. From there, it will take a lot of probing to make him concede and agree that perhaps he may have had a role in his own misfortune.

Who are you more like? Do you look outwards for *excuses* or inwards for *reasons*? When was the last time you gave yourself honest feedback? This process is all about asking yourself the right questions. My first client was not asking himself the right questions. He was not asking himself any questions.

His story centred on blaming others. The shift begins by looking within first and figuring out what you could have proactively done to achieve your goal. It could be that you were indeed powerless to change things. The point however is this: The question must come *before* the conclusion.

The statements below are examples of shifts in feedback from conclusion to question:

It's wasn't my fault.	Could I have done more?
My day was ruined.	Did I allow it to ruin my day?
I was very upset.	Do I have good reason to be upset?

If you put the conclusion first, you are choking off any constructive feedback available to you. You'll notice that all the statements relate to the past. Feedback is based on something that has actually happened. Looking back at the event is like playing an old film to recreate what you experienced and felt at the time.

There is a trap we can fall into, especially if we decide to take the narrow view of what happened. The mind is a wonderful tool but not without limitations. If you don't make a conscious effort to focus on what actually happened, you leave yourself open to drifting, to conflating imagination and reality. It's so easy to cloud the experience with what you *thought* happened as opposed to what *really* happened. This is why being open to feedback from the start is important, because you are more in heart space, as you feel the emotions. It is also important not to be overrun by these emotions and lose the opportunity to grow and learn from the situation. Try to be objective by engaging some head space into this.

It's important too to feedback while in the moment, while the memory is still clear. The alternative is to take it all into your head space and reframe and edit it until you have a version that backs up your claims, just like my first client.

Failure is Feedback

My biggest business failure was a very big failure, by any standards. Here's what happened. I was made redundant in the depths of the financial crisis, and decided to take the plunge and set up a race organisation business. It was a very risky decision, but by this time I was beginning to listen more closely to my own passions. I had always really wanted to work for myself and I was determined to make it happen.

For 13 months, I worked 12-hour days organising my marquee event, the Eireman Triathlon in my home county of Wexford. The logistics that went into this were extensive. I worked with everyone from the local authorities to the Gardaí to Fáilte Ireland and any number of community agencies. I had a three-year plan which aimed to make Eireman the biggest triathlon in the country. For those 13 months, I eked out my meagre redundancy money and lived like a pauper. Don't get me wrong, I was happy, I was thrilled to be fully engaged in trying to make my dream a reality, but it was tough work.

Entries were coming in slowly, so I decided that I needed to add a half-Ironman distance. When this didn't improve things significantly, I added the Olympic distance. Things improved, but not enough, so I decided to go the whole hog and add the sprint distance too. Momentum began to build. I went to triathlons all over the country to drum up interest. I flew to the UK, hired a car and took a stand at an important sports trade show. I didn't have the money for a hotel, so I slept in the car, and would you believe it, it snowed. I'll never forget how cold that night was.

I flew in the editor of the world's biggest triathlon magazine to cover the event, and as the day approached, everything started to come together. The night before the race, I was interviewed on RTÉ's *Six*

One News about it. It was just after the news, when the weather forecast came on, that I realised there could be trouble ahead. A storm. An honest to God storm. In August. What's more, it was headed straight for Courtown, straight for the start of the race.

I didn't get any sleep that night because I was out setting up the traffic diversion signs after a helper called in sick. As dawn broke, I knew we had serious problems. There was wind, there was rain, it was cold, and worst of all, the sea was rough. Very rough. The weird thing was, there was no storm in Dublin, and further south in Wexford, there was little sign of it either. It just remained unmoving overhead, pounding Courtown harbour. So I sat down with the coastguard and the technical delegates from Triathlon Ireland who were assigned to my race and discussed what we would do.

Ultimately, they left it up to me. After as much soul searching as the timetable would allow, I decided to cancel the swim and replace it with a run. I don't regret taking that decision. There would have been plenty of competitors who looked at the water and thought to themselves, 'I could swim in that, no problem'. But you have to think of the weakest swimmers. You have to think of those who are competing for the first time. I knew then that even if everything went perfectly from that moment on, the absence of a swim was a very big negative mark against my key event, and therefore my business.

Now, instead of swim, bike, run, it became a run, bike, run – for four separate races. We had to create four new runs for each race at really short notice, while out on the course conditions were getting worse and worse all the time. Delays left competitors waiting in the wind-driven rain for far too long, turning bad moods into really bad moods. Communications broke down, and on one section of the course, a small set of runners were directed the wrong way.

Meanwhile, the traffic management plan – which had to go smoothly to give me any hope of getting the go-ahead for future races – fell apart. The implementation of the diversions left some people stranded in their cars for hours at a time. It was a disaster. I had people queuing up to give me abuse, all of which I took. I was accused of all kinds of things by people who had trusted me to deliver a well-organised event. And the following Tuesday, the local press got stuck in and made it front page news. It was horrible. Thinking about it still gives me the shivers.

Okay, it wasn't my fault that the weather forced the cancellation of the swim, but it was my fault that I didn't have sufficient manpower to deal with the enforced changes. It was my fault that I didn't have a Plan B ready. What I realised, once the dust had settled, was that my business model was flawed. To run a full scale, economically viable Ironman event, I needed more manpower, and yet there were insufficient revenue in such a business – in Ireland anyway – to justify hiring more people. The other major lesson was that I should have had a Plan B ready to take off the shelf when it was needed, instead of having to cobble one together at the last minute. Triathlon Ireland saw this too, and since then, they insist that all events have a Plan B, if and when conditions force the cancelation of a swim.

It was a nightmarish experience. That evening, I was so tired, so demoralised and so just plain upset that I wished the sea would swallow me up. But it didn't. I kept going with the business. The Eireman episode became a teacher – a big brute of a teacher with a large stick – but a teacher nonetheless. Less than a month later, I had planned an off-road triathlon in the same location. I could have cancelled it, reimbursed everyone and gone off and hid under a rock, but I didn't. I went ahead with it – and with what felt like half the world watching – I pulled it off. It went great, and so too did all the many races I organised since then. I now have a thriving business, and when something goes wrong – as it inevitably does – I'm ready for it. I deal with it. Don't get me wrong, I still wish Eireman hadn't gone so badly wrong, but has that

experience lead to success? Unquestionably.

Internal Feedback

Feedback can be instantaneous. Have you ever asked yourself 'How do I feel right now?'. Close your eyes and ask yourself the question. Feeling good – I hope. We tend to only really focus on how we feel when we are down in the dumps. So here's a challenge: feedback to yourself when you are really happy. Don't just think about feeling happy using your head space; try and bring heart space into it. Close your eyes and concentrate on how you actually **feel** when you are really happy. Do this a few times until you sense the feelings of happiness rising within you.

If you'd asked me to do this a few years ago, I'd have been stuck because when I was happy, I never paid much attention to the feeling. I was in the flow of happiness, so I was consciously incompetent. But when it came to recounting a feeling of unhappiness, I could tap into the feeling effortlessly. In an instant, I could become consciously competent of sadness. I wonder if you can relate to this. It's not a revelation that people struggle to feedback their feelings of happiness to themselves. If you never took time out during a moment of happiness to consciously feel it, how can you accurately record the experience? It might seem strange that some people can't remember how it is to feel genuinely happy. If we can plug easily into sadness, then shouldn't we be able to plug into happiness in just the same way?

To do this, simply plan to take time out the next time you are really feeling happy, so you can experience consciously what is going on. Feel the feelings. Ask yourself what they feel like. Record specific pictures in your mind. Become aware of what you are hearing. See if you can intensify it. When you are finished creating this memory, write it down. Next day, go back to the same place in your mind and run through the same routine. Repeat this regularly and you'll develop a first-class ticket to always feeling happy.

The Runner's Rhyme

Running gives you one of the best opportunities to engage your internal feedback system. I call this simple little feedback tool the 'Runner's Rhyme'. I've had so many clients – as well as those with whom I've shared this system online – feedback about how much it's helped them. You're in a 10mile/km race. You're coming up to the 7 mile mark. This is usually the point where it begins to hurt and energy starts to wane. I describe it as the limbo section of a race. This too is where the voices tend to kick in.

'Slow down.'

'You're not fit enough.'

'You'll never beat that person beside you.'

'You're not going to finish. What were you thinking, entering this race?'

If those thoughts/voices start to dominate your thinking, it can be really hard to ignore or dampen them. Instead, replace them with the Runner's Rhyme. It goes like this:

'I look good, I sound good, I feel good.'

REPEAT

'I look good, I sound good, I feel good.'

Repeat. And keep repeating – only do it quietly to yourself, so no one will think you're nuts. Or, if it helps, do repeat it out loud, and let them think you're nuts as you run past them. They probably won't chase after you as a result.

There is some theory behind this tool. Early research suggests that human beings can be conscious of a maximum of seven thoughts at any one time. More recent research suggests we can be conscious of four thoughts. I guess it's probably somewhere in between, but let's just assume it's seven for the moment. So that mantra, 'I look good, I sound good, I feel good' takes up three of those seven slots. You have also to be conscious of running in a straight line and not bumping into others. That's four. Obeying stewards and looking for kilometre signs or for your supporters makes five thoughts. Your sixth thought could be checking out the other runners around you. Who are you marking? Who do you want to beat? The seventh thought I'll leave up to you. Maybe it's visualising the finish line. When your conscious mind is busy like that, there's simply no room for negative thoughts.

For the Runner's Rhyme to be really effective, you must drill down into the three layers of how you look, sound and feel. This is proper internal feedback. This drill-down method will dominate your conscious mind. It will be a primary thought which distracts you while you move along the course. Keeping yourself focused with the Runner's Rhyme allows little room for those negative voices.

'I look good.'

To be clear, looking good is not about how your mascara is holding up or how you'll appear in the race photos. Both may be important but they're secondary concerns compared with your posture. Sure, you're tired. But if you allow your mind to hit a wall of negative thoughts, your body will complement those thoughts and act accordingly. So do a quick posture check:

> My head – Is it in a position where my eyes are looking forward and not down?
>
> My back – Is it in my normal running posture?
>
> My knees – Am I raising them?
>
> My feet – Am I light on my feet or pounding?

If everything is okay, carry on. If not, take corrective action. And remember that you can check all of this much quicker than it took to read.

'I sound good.'

Listen to your breathing and heart rate. Are you breathing like a bull and your heart about to explode from your chest? Maybe you need to hold back a little. If you're unsure, get a watch with a heart rate monitor to assist you. It will bleep if you're pushing too hard.

'I feel good.'

Time for a complete body drill. This is self-scanning out on the course. Firstly, I identify the part of the body. Then I ask the question 'feeling good'? To which I'll answer yes or no.

Top of my head – feeling good?

Neck – feeling good?

Chest – feeling good?

Arms – feeling good?

My stomach – feeling good?

My hips – feeling good?

My glutes – feeling good?

My hamstrings – feeling good?

My quads – feeling good?

My calves – feeling good?

My shins – feeling good?

My Achilles – feeling good?

My feet – feeling good?

Feel free to add or omit any parts you feel appropriate! Performing the complete scan will distract you for at least 100 metres. If something doesn't feel good, I always try and give it some positive energy. Send it down some love. Tell it it's doing a great job and that you're really grateful for its contribution. And then, when you return to the 'I feel good' section of the Runner's Rhyme later in the course, monitor anything that didn't pass the previous check. It goes without saying of course that if you are in serious pain, it might be best to pull up and live to fight another day.

The Runner's Rhyme works for beginners, intermediate and advanced runners. And remember that your description of how you feel doesn't have to be limited to 'good'. Why not 'great', 'awesome' or 'outstanding'? The rhyme is an opportunity to pump in motivational descriptors of how you feel. And remember too that the language you use will have an influence on how you feel. Thoughts become things. And we can further enhance this with a memory loop.

A Memory Loop

I want you to read this next piece slowly because I'm going to explain how to make yourself consciously competent of feeling great, and how to recreate those great feelings at will.

First of all, you need to genuinely feel the happiness within you. Think of some great moment in your life. Then feed back to yourself what this happiness is doing for you. Take your time over this. Remember the event, then do something else completely unrelated for one minute to take your mind away from it.

Now I want you to once again remember this happy sensation. Close your eyes. Recreate it with all five senses. Remember where you were, what you felt, what smells were in the air, what were the sights and sounds. Remember it all. Stay with the memory, except now I want you to make the scene bigger, the colours more radiant, the sounds louder.

While you are imagining this, I want you to touch your thumb and index finger (beside your thumb) together. I suggest you use the hand you don't write with. Hold the thumb and finger together and imagine the great scene of happiness in front of you. Repeat this several times using the same or different happy memories. If you use the same memory, move around the scene and watch from different angles to freshen it up.

Repeat this every day. And soon enough, by squeezing your thumb and index finger together, your mind will drift back to the sensation. We are creatures of habit. Just as a hot drink can be associated with burning your tongue, so too can happiness and finger squeezing. You have created a memory loop, or trigger, which will always remind you of what happiness feels like.

The Memory Loop in Action

I did some work with a golfer who wanted to turn pro. His form had dipped substantially in the previous few months, not least because of a range of what he termed 'external distractions'. We looked at all those factors, simply to acknowledge them, but what I wanted to know was what had changed in his game – what were the things he used to do when he was playing well that he no longer did. Call them his 'controllables'. We talked about these for some time before be revealed that he had dropped his signature trigger exercise. Back when he was playing well, he used to pull on his glove and say to himself 'Let's get busy'. This was a wonderful little move, and each time it proved very helpful in getting him into the zone. But somewhere along the way, he forgot it. He dropped it. Getting him to re-establish that ritual was central to his subsequent return to form.

You can use the same kind of ritual for running. Think of the best race you ever ran. Go back to the sensations you felt that day. Work through the steps above and bring yourself into that zone again. Create a new physical experience with your hand (if contact between thumb and index finger already has a role). It needs to be some form of contact you can sustain until the sensation has been programmed that won't take you off your stride. Maybe make a fist or whatever works best for you.

Feedback exercise

I would like you to feedback/score how you are doing in seven areas of your life. Please ensure you add the date so it captures the present moment. If there are any important areas that need to be worked on, make them your priority. I would then encourage you to score it again in two months' time to check your progress.

Date _____

Rainbow Life Test®

On a scale of 1 to 10 (10 being excellent), where are you now with?

Peace of mind   1   2   3   4   5   6   7   8   9   10

Health and energy   1   2   3   4   5   6   7   8   9   10

**Family/
relationships**   1   2   3   4   5   6   7   8   9   10

Financial freedom   1   2   3   4   5   6   7   8   9   10

**Achieving a
challenging goal**   1   2   3   4   5   6   7   8   9   10

**Personal
development**   1   2   3   4   5   6   7   8   9   10

Overall happiness   1   2   3   4   5   6   7   8   9   10

Outcome Running: Getting Your Thoughts in Order

Failure does not define you. Sometimes your training will not go to plan. Sometimes you won't reach your target time in a race. Feedback on what went well and what didn't. Keep a training diary, to allow you to recall what worked and what didn't, plus all the externals.

A training diary – like a gratitude diary – can help you to stay focused. The endless churn of thoughts and plans and whims and notions through our heads can make it difficult to think about what we need to think about. This is why I like to write things down. It makes it so much easier to disentangle my thoughts and retain everything that needs to be retained. Feedback to yourself using the Runner's Rhyme. 'I look good' – check your posture. 'I sound good' – listen to your breathing. 'I feel good' – body scan from head to toe. And remember, why stop with good? How about excellent? Or magnificent!

Action Steps

1. Failure is only failure if you learn nothing from it. Allow all failure to become feedback. Be honest! Be slow to find externals to blame, and feedback quickly, when your memory of the event is at its freshest and it's harder to fool yourself about what really happened.
2. Next time you feel genuinely happy, take the time to notice it.
3. Practise the memory loop and use it for running/happiness. Remember the golfer who said 'Let's get busy'. When you lace up your runners, you can trigger your own memory loop.

Running Tip

Try to vary the surfaces that you run on. Most people run on four types of surface: concrete, tarmac, treadmill or grass. Concrete, unfortunately, is the most common surface, and is also the most unforgiving. There is no 'bounce' from concrete, so repeated training on it can lead to injury. And the longer you can stay injury-free the stronger/faster you will become. Grass is the best surface for runners. Woodland trails and soft earth are a close second and third, respectively. You can't go too far wrong running around football pitches as the surface is bound to be reasonably flat – with no surprise holes. Of course, the novelty of this might wear off quickly.

I suggest variety. Depending on where you live, you might have access to all four surfaces or more. Hard sand can also give you a nice bounce if you live near the coast. Check out your surroundings and plan your runs. I make sure to mix grass with path on my long runs. If I see some grass, I'll run on it (provided it isn't part of a golf course...).

Racing Tip

Make sure to congratulate yourself first when you finish a race. Here is an opportunity to feedback to yourself when you feel genuinely happy (after you catch your breath). Then, if they are still vertical, congratulate the people you finished with. But primarily tell yourself how well you did in that moment before reporting on social media or looking to congratulate friends. Give yourself credit. Be your own biggest supporter.

Isn't it great to be that person crossing the finish line? You are now *that person*! You made this happen. What a gift it is to be able to get yourself around a course with so many other enthusiastic people. This may be your first time or you may be an experienced runner with a new PB (personal best). Enjoy the positive feelings. Savour them. Think of it this way: if I don't support and congratulate myself, why should I expect anyone else to?

The Fifth Milestone – Significance

My first Ironman race was Ironman Austria. A full Ironman is a triathlon consisting of a 3.8km swim, a 180km cycle and finishing with a marathon. I remember being at the competitor's village, I was queuing up to get my bike examined by the mechanic the day before the race. There was a long queue but it was worth it to get the bike checked; I knew that it had taken a lot of punishment on the airplane. Looking around, one thing was very clear to me; my bike was very much on the mediocre side. Everyone else seemed to have a flashy, high-priced bike. I didn't.

When it came to my turn, the mechanic took one look at it, made a kind of a snorting noise and waved for the person behind me to come forward. I didn't speak German but I stood my ground and signalled that it was my turn. There was a standoff and finally he sighed heavily, took it and heaved it reluctantly up onto the plinth. Did I feel insignificant? Not one bit. I thought it was funny. The next day I finished in the top third of the field, miles ahead of the many bikes that were way better than mine.

Sometimes we cheat ourselves out of feeling significance; you see someone with a pair of high-priced running shoes, a pair of compression socks and a running club singlet and automatically think they are faster than you. The truth of course is that you just don't know how fast they are. You don't know the first thing about them. Feeling insignificant is a self-imposed prison sentence. It cuts you off from being your whole self. True significance lies in focusing on what you have, not on what you don't have.

Significant Heroes

It is of course important to have heroes and people you admire. The danger lies in picking the wrong people, and for the wrong reasons. Choose to admire people's achievements rather than to envy their success. And I'm not saying you shouldn't have aspirations to emulate those whom you admire; that is important. But the danger is that you find yourself in a state of perpetual want, which makes you unable to enjoy the present moment. Your grounded significance happens in the present moment. You may think to yourself that you'll feel significant when you get this or own that. If you are always thinking in the future and your focus is solely on future gratification, you are postponing life. Equally, if you are living with a lingering feeling of insignificance, you are negating your present happiness. It will catch you both ways, so it needs to be addressed.

Be yourself, everyone else is taken.

Much of this work will be done in the final section of the book, when we talk about goals: goals designed to deliver both present and future happiness.

Unemployed = insignificant?

I can remember how demoralised and insignificant I felt when I was made redundant. I know I'm not alone in this. Having meaningful work is a fundamental component of wellbeing. Back then, however, I knew nothing about self-help or positivity. All I knew was that if I sat at home and did nothing, it would be really difficult to get my energy levels up to a point where I would do a good interview. So I decided to do two things: (a) vigorously apply for jobs and (b) get fit. I had played hurling throughout my teenage years, but a hand injury when I was 17 put those days behind me. I took up jogging after that, but I did it without any real heart, just to kill time and stay lean. When I ran, I ran the same boring old loop all the time. To try to inspire myself, and to take things up a notch, I joined a triathlon club. At that first session, I talked to three lads who were getting ready for an Ironman. I didn't even know what it was at that time, but when they explained it, I was smitten. I had to get involved. I just had to!

There were however two immediate problems. I didn't have a bike and I couldn't swim. The first problem was easily remedied. The second took a little more work, not least because I was phobic about the water. But the one thing I did have was time. I took lessons, and in the following months, I was in the pool every other day practising. Aided by the experts at the triathlon club, I put a great training programme together, and within a year, I was capable of doing a half-Ironman– which included a 1.9km swim.

Getting fit was great, and it really stood to me in the years ahead, but you can't train all day, so after a few weeks I realised I needed something else *significant* in my life – something that would keep me sharp, something to make me feel like I mattered. So I had a longer, deeper think about what I'd done in the past and what had made me feel significant, what had made me feel like I had something to offer.

The one thing that stood out was working with people with disabilities in Argentina.

I already had the necessary experience, so I applied for part-time work at Saint John of God Hospital, Dublin, working with adults with disabilities. The work was much the same as the work in Argentina, and we had an arrangement whereby I could go for interviews when they cropped up. It was great. It was just great – taking people out, feeding them, looking after them, entertaining them. The whole thing sparked me back to life. I felt I was making a contribution to the world, a significant contribution, instead of just sitting on the couch, waiting for a job to appear.

(If you're ever in need of a pick-me-up, if you ever feel unsure about your place in the world, go help someone out. You have to give a lot when you help people with disabilities, but you get twice as much back in return!) And, ultimately, because I was in such a great frame of mind, it didn't take long to get myself the job I wanted. Should you find yourself facing a change in life like unemployment, be mindful of not allowing it to swallow up all your significance. Find other ways to bolster your significance so it isn't dependent on just one part of your life.

Make your contribution to the world NOW. Nobody remembers what you thought about doing.

Eoin Ryan

Intrinsic and Extrinsic Significance

Intrinsic significance is about placing a value on internally satisfying elements. These could include personal development goals, possessions and experiences. You do these things or acquire these things for **you** (and it doesn't really matter what others think). Acquiring or reaching them will build up your intrinsic significance. Reading this book and adopting its ideas into your life will enhance your intrinsic significance. I guarantee it. Extrinsic significance, by contrast, is about putting a value on externals such as status and approval from others. For example, you might share on social media what you intend to do or what you have already done or bought. Being recognised favourably by our peers has a feel-good factor. Maybe you bought this book so you could help improve your personal best time in a race. Then you'll be able to beat your running friends in races.

Both intrinsic and extrinsic significance have an important place in our lives. I always factor in a mix of both when I prepare my goals. When I trained for the seven marathons in six days, the Austrian Ironman and the Marathon des Sables, I used this same pattern. Firstly, I wrote down why this goal would make me feel intrinsically significant. Then I would write down why it would make me feel extrinsically significant. I'm a big believer of leading with intrinsically significant gains. Or at least, on balance, try to be more intrinsically biased. Why? I believe that the significance and enjoyment lasts longer if you are intrinsically biased. Most people who know me will have forgotten that I achieved some or all of my significant goals. I'm cool with that because that extrinsic significance was not my main motivation for doing them. I'm still very much enjoying them intrinsically.

Take the example of someone running their first marathon. Their sole intrinsic reason for doing this is to fulfil an ambition to complete a marathon. Their extrinsic reasons may be numerous: to run faster than a friend, to come in under three hours, to win a bet and silence their doubters on social media. Now, this may work and this person may indeed succeed, but making a point to elevate yourself above others doesn't really have as much longevity as the internal significance you could foster from doing it.

What if no one really cared that you succeeded? That would negate a large proportion of your significance. Find out what it is that makes you feel significant. In my own case, when I was unemployed, I had a narrow range of choices. I'm sure you will have many more. And don't just go looking for sources of significance in times of upheaval. Set out to do it when things are going well.

In the previous chapter, I talked about keeping a Gratitude Journal. Now, I would ask you to add a new section to that journal. Start to record all the things that make you feel significant. We can be blind to these sometimes. We can tend simply to compare ourselves with others and decide that we want what they have. This is the 'far away hills are greener' mentality. The truth is that the sum of all the small things combined will show you just how significant you are. You could divide this section in your journal into intrinsic and extrinsic significance.

Remember, self-help is about small shifts. We may never be perfect and that isn't expected. Eliminating negatives such as feeling insignificant is a step towards bringing much more positivity into your life. Cataloguing your levels of significance allows you to focus on how significant you already are. Perhaps more than you imagined. Life, as we all know, is full of ups and downs. The more work you put into improving your positivity levels, the better you'll be able to deal with volatility. You'll have the reserves built up (similar to training and building up the stamina for a race) so that when adversity comes your way the work you have done on increasing your levels of positivity will stand to you.

We'll be talking more about significance a little later on in the final section of the book, when we look at setting goals. It is important to state before we get there, however, that if you are not willing to set out a plan, to work hard and make sacrifices, those feelings of insignificance could remain. Put in the work to bolster those feelings of significance now.

Do a Marathon

Seriously, if you haven't already, start training for a marathon. You can run a marathon almost anywhere these days. At the North Pole, the Great Wall of China or even at home on a treadmill watching soaps on TV. Completing a marathon does wonders for your levels of significance – and it's a lot more achievable than you think. With the exception of the people chasing prize money, everyone who completes the marathon holds equal status. Everyone gets their time, their medal, their goodie bag. You don't even have to run it. Once you've walked it, you can tick it off your bucket list.

At a brisk pace, you might walk one mile in 20 minutes, taking you just under nine hours to walk 26.2 miles. Walking a 15-minute mile, you would finish 26.2 miles in under seven hours. When I suggest walking it, the standard response I get is 'I want to *run* it'. Apparently, there is less significance associated with walking it. Did you know that? I doubt that the walkers who cover the 26.2 miles would agree. Training to run a marathon all the way, non-stop is a much bigger commitment than walking it. Because of that, many of those who want to complete their first marathon as a runner will never do it. They will deny themselves an amazing experience because of this curious perception that walking it isn't significant enough.

Ask yourself, does that way of thinking belong in my life? Am I putting significance ahead of experience? Or am I just using significance to deflect laziness? Tough questions. Do they make you think of something that you've wanted to do but have been holding off doing? Keep that example for goal setting in the final section of this book. Put the book down for a second please and have a think about that. The marathon example relates back to our self-imposed prisons. What do you value more: extrinsic significance or intrinsic significance? What others think of me and what I do or have or what I think of myself and what I do or have?

There is a joke that goes around that tells you a lot about human nature and significance.

Question: At a wedding, how would you know if someone has done an Ironman triathlon?

Answer: They'll be sure to tell you.

An extrinsically significant conversation. I'm guilty of it too by the way! Of course, it is great to tell people about your achievements, but for a more lasting impact on your wellbeing, intrinsic significance has to be your first priority. Do I feel significant because I'm dressed up in the best running clothes and have a satellite watch or because I beat the guy with all the running 'bling'? Significance, and how you measure it, is a very subjective thing – and a deceptive thing too. Think of your job status. You may take great significance from what you do, and you may believe that others regard you highly because of it, but the truth is that some people would hate your job. The things that are significant in your life someone else might run a hundred miles from!

SIGNIFICANCE

Stage 1

For the majority of time, do you feel significant or insignificant? Mark it on the scale below

Significant   Insignificant

|----------|----------|----------|----------|----------|

2   1   0   1   2

Stage 2

Outline three examples that make you feel significant   ____   ____
Outline three examples that make you feel insignificant   ____   ____

Write a paragraph on **why** each of the three makes you feel insignificant.
From the insignificant examples, circle the ones you have power to change.
(If you can't change them, I suggest they are taking up unnecessary headspace)

Taking the six examples in Stage 2, put a tick beside the ones that are intrinsically based
and a circle around the ones that are extrinsically based.

_____

Outcome question: Are you over indexing on external things to define your significance? Take
a deeper look and write down some more internal things. _____

_____

Outcome Running: Getting Your Thoughts in Order

Running automatically makes you significant. It demonstrates that you are making a positive decision regarding the health and wellbeing of your body. It shows you have love for yourself through exercising. Those of us who chase extrinsic significance will always want to win the race. We believe we have been given significance by those who have seen us triumph. This kind of significance is dependent on others. But what if nobody is looking? What happens to your significance then? First and foremost, build your intrinsic significance.

It doesn't matter if you are a slow runner or can only run in spurts. If you feel internally significant about your progress, that is all that matters. Avoid the comparison trap; that's your ticket to insignificance. Focus on what you have going for you. The things that make you who you are: a deeply significant person.

Action Steps

1. Beware of the comparison trap when it comes to feeling significant. Unlock your significance prison and remind yourself of how significant you are.
2. Aim for intrinsically significant things above extrinsically significant things. That gives you firmer ground to stand on by yourself.
3. Put completing a marathon on your goal list. Walking or running.

Running Tip

You don't need the best, most up-to-date, most expensive running gear to feel significant. It's not about what's cool or 'in' this season. It's about what's comfortable and what works. When I ran the Marathon des Sables, I didn't get a single blister on my feet. Blisters are the bane of most competitors and can even end your race. People go to great lengths to harden their feet. I've heard all kinds of old wives' tales about the best way to avoid blisters, including filing your feet using sandpaper or an emery board, or soaking them in paraffin oil. I just trained in an old pair of double layer socks. Sure, they were a bit grey after 300+ washes but it worked. New socks every month? I don't think so.

When it comes to running shoes, it's more about comfort and support than what brand you wear. Go to a running specialist shop; they have the expertise. Tell them what you intend to do. For shoes, get a gait analysis done. When buying clothes or socks, avoid cotton products. Any material that draws away sweat is what you need. The value of getting the correct gear for long runs cannot be overstated.

Racing Tip

Lots of races have signs or pens dedicated to runners who want to finish the race with a target time in mind. For example in a half marathon there might be a section for those who wish to finish in 1 hr 30 mins, 1 hr 45 mins, 2 hrs, etc. If the race is timed using timing chips (most are), there is no advantage beginning in the front row of the race with the elites unless you are planning on finishing among the elites.

Starting the race behind others does not diminish your significance. In fact, the opposite is true. If you start in a pen that is too ambitious for you, you'll feel rather insignificant when everyone is running past you. Personally, I prefer to be competing against people who are the same speed as me rather than being continuously passed out. So start in a pen that reflects your current abilities. Set a future target to train hard so you can start in a quicker pen. Road racing doesn't have as much etiquette as golf but this would be a top three point. Any slower runners ahead of you have to be passed, which can slow you down or block your path. Not cool.

The Sixth Milestone– Generosity

On the fourth day of running seven marathons in six days along the canals of Ireland, my pre-planning came unstuck. And what a day for it to happen, too. This was my double marathon day (84km) and it was raining so heavily that every sporting event in the country had been cancelled – except mine. It had been a late decision to start in Longford town rather than the official start on the Royal Canal at Cloondara. The logic was that we'd get a better response to bucket collections in a town rather than a village. Unfortunately, I never gave the updated itinerary and maps to the support crew. They had the old versions, which still had the start of the run in Cloondara.

The canal is not flanked continuously by roads, so I had to mark the meeting points for food stops and general meeting points on maps. Naturally, the crew would follow my instructions; it had worked perfectly until now. But as a consequence of me not giving them the updated maps, they'd gone to the wrong meeting point on another section of the canal. To make matters worse, I was alone on the first leg and hadn't brought a phone with me. I had decided to leave it in the support vehicle as it would have been destroyed by the pelting rain. I was *incommunicado*.

This leg of the adventure was also the most remote. So remote that the towpath of the canal was not maintained. I ran though nettles, briars, over gates and under fences. I had to guess which was the right side of the canal to be on. I got it wrong once and hit a dead end, then decided to jump in the canal and swim across rather than retreat a few kilometres to a bridge. I was soaked to the bone anyway, so it didn't matter.

When I arrived at the updated meeting point, the support crew were nowhere to be seen. I waited for ten minutes until I began shivering and knew that I had to keep moving if I didn't want the cold to really kick in. A few kilometres further on, I reached the next checkpoint, where the road and canal met. There was still no sign of my crew. Now I was beginning to worry. I had no food, no water, no phone and was in the process of running a double marathon. If I didn't eat soon, the challenge would be over and all my hard work wasted.

I hadn't passed a house for a few kilometres and there were none at this checkpoint, so once again, I had no choice but to carry on. About 3km further on, I finally came to a cottage and knocked on the door. No answer. It was, I realised, an empty summer cottage. I began to suspect in this part of the run that was all I was likely to come across. I kept going, but by now I was starting to feel very fatigued and very anxious.

A kilometre or so later I come to another house. This time, there was smoke coming from the chimney. Someone was home. I knocked on the door. As I waited for an answer, I looked down at my legs. They were badly cut and bleeding from the briars. My runners were covered in mud from pulling myself out of the canal. I was soaked to the bone. I looked destitute. An old man answered the door. He looked me up and down and asked, 'Did you have an accident?' I explained the situation and asked if I could use his phone. I managed to get through to the crew, and with his help, gave them a location where they could come to meet me. They were a long way away, confused and worried. Then, with one question, this man became my hero. He asked 'Would you like something to eat?' Would I what?!

He opened his fridge and fed a starving runner. Sandwiches never tasted so good! Then he recalled that he saw me being interviewed on TV about the run. Funny – I think he had only half-believed me up to then. Next thing, he was on the phone telling all the houses along the canal for the next 10Km to look out for me and the support crew. Meanwhile, I'm eating everything that he puts on the table. His generosity saved my challenge. There was certainly no way I could have finished it without this stranger's help. That's the magic of generosity.

A Giving Cycle

We are all naturally programmed to be givers. Go back to our caveman friend; if he hadn't shared the meat from the kill, the human race would be extinct. Sharing is in our nature. People who are takers are missing out on the tremendous benefits of giving. I'm not talking here about the status you get from being seen to give – that is very much head space thinking. Imagine what your world would be like if you spent your time thinking of what you could do for other people rather than wonder what everyone can do for you. How does that sound to you?

I, like many others, have done things and never received thanks for them. But that is operating from the position of 'giving to receive', the head space zone. When I learned about the distinction between head and heart space, it created a shift in my thinking. Old me would be upset I didn't get thanked. New me doesn't mind. If you are being generous and giving from the heart space, you don't need a 'thank you'. It isn't necessary. You have created enough wholesome energy in your body (call it karma) by giving to supersede any gesture of gratitude, forthcoming or not. You have played your role brilliantly. If others don't respond in kind, it doesn't reduce the karma you have acquired. You stop playing your role brilliantly when you focus on what you didn't receive rather than what you did. In fact, you spoil your own party. Have a think about this.

We don't all have the time to go out and volunteer, though if you do make the time, you will find it a wonderfully enriching experience, one which sits very much in the heart space zone. There are lots of other things you can do to experience the joy of giving. Give your time, give someone who needs it a listening ear, or even give a hug. Think about all the stuff you hoard, the things sitting unused in the attic or the garage or the bottom of the wardrobe. How many things do you have lying around that will never be used again? Why not give away what you are happy to give away? Remember that you are not giving to receive. This is total heart space generosity. Once you have your pile in order, I suggest you bring it to a charity shop. Why? You don't need to know who gets it because you don't need any thanks. If you simply give it to a friend, you might warp the heart space and go to head space by thinking they owe you a favour. Take a look online and learn something about the work that the charity does. You have contributed to this work. Once you have decided what you are going to give using your heart space, let go and enjoy the journey. Generosity is a heart space gift. It shines a light that emanates from you, not on you.

GENEROSITY

Stage 1

When you were generous in the past – which 'space' mostly describes your motives?
Please circle

Head space   or   Heart space

Recall a head space and heart space example. What was the main difference between them?
Head space example _____   Heart space example _____
The difference _____

Stage 2

Expand on how you can be more generous to others in some of these areas:

Your Time	Possessions	Money	Encouragement

Outcome question: Next time you give something - work purely from heart space and log
your feelings here

The Karma of Giving

I organise road-running races on the east coast of Ireland. I remember the first Wexford Half-Marathon and Relay very clearly. As the name suggests, there was a relay element to the event. The buses transporting the relay participants to the changeover points left from the main starting area. We had advertised the departure times for the two buses extensively before the event, and I also announced those times regularly over the loudspeaker that morning. When the time came, I was relieved and delighted to see the buses rolling out on time. Job done. Five minutes later, a young guy came up to me and asked where were the buses. When I told him they were gone, he was aghast.

'What? This is terrible! The other guys on my team need me to be at the changeover point in time!'

I was up to my neck in jobs so I couldn't drive him. I suggested he catch a taxi, but he told me he had no money. I reached for my wallet and all I had was €20. This was double what he needed, but I gave it to him, smiled and got on with my mountain of jobs. This was the first time we organised the race in Wexford, and it went great. Everything that could go right went right. I put that down to that gesture with this guy. I fully believe being generous and giving out good karma had a big influence on its success. I never heard from him again; that doesn't bother me in the slightest.

> *We make a living by what we get, we make*
> *a life by what we give.*
>
> Winston Churchill

The Generosity Spark

I mentioned in the introduction that the idea for this book was sparked by the spontaneous generosity you get when you take part in road races. The claps, the cheers, the high fives you get from the people lining the route give you a wonderful injection of positive energy when you run. You forget how tired and sore you are. This is a very tangible example of how generosity delivers, how uplifting it can be. Say 'thank you' if you can. High five back; participate in this wonderful exchange of generosity with total strangers. Now imagine how you could replicate that uplifting feeling along the whole racecourse and eliminate all the negative thoughts. Wouldn't that make things easier? Do you think you might go faster? Could you replicate the same feelings in everyday life?

The answer to all those questions is yes.

You are now over halfway through the *Outcome Running* milestones. Every step forward from this point is a step closer to your goal. When this journey is over, you may want to revisit some of the exercises just to see how things may have changed for you. The exercises are designed to catch how you are feeling at that particular moment. Gauge your progress by completing them again.

We create our futures in the present moment. Today is the day. There will never be a perfect time. Perfection can be a success assassin. A leap from the starting blocks to perfection is impossible, especially if you're just finding your feet. Goals must be broken into chunks to sustain your motivation. We'll talk more about this in the final section of the book.

Outcome Running: Getting Your Thoughts in Order

Have you ever considered giving something back to your running group or your wider community? Many of you might already be in clubs or groups. Most athletic clubs have an annual club race. Could you help in some way? I hire marshals from athletic clubs for my races. I know how hard it can be to get people to commit to helping. (I've attended some of those pre-race meetings.)

If or when the opportunity arises, will you 'put your hand up instead of your putting your hand out'? That is how I became a race organiser. Nobody wanted to be race director for our triathlon race. I volunteered and the rest is history. You'll never know how your generosity might be repaid or what life skills or friends you will gain. Being generous with your time holds true for 'you time' as well. Make sure you get your runs in. Sometimes that might mean going to bed earlier to get up earlier and run. Eight hours' sleep is more than enough per night.

Action Steps

1. Gather together all the things you no longer use and give them to charity.
2. One of the most important accounts you have is your karma account. Make a deposit every day.
3. When you give, give from heart space. Don't expect anything in return. Observe just how good it makes you feel.

Running Tip

Many runners say that running is their therapy. It's their time out. It's their opportunity to process events in their lives. It is a time to be out in nature. And some people will say that it's none of these things. Maybe they are just running to stay fit. Plain and simple.

I'll make a bet with you that the people who aren't experiencing all those peripheral pleasures from running are carrying electronic devices with them. In other words, they are either distracted by music or consumed by time-keeping on their watches. There's nothing wrong with this, of course, but I do suggest that you leave the gizmos at home from time to time. Try running 'electronically naked' for a change. Listen to your heart beating rather than the watch bleeps. Tune into nature's stereo rather than swiping through your playlists. It is my belief that the smarter technology gets, the less grounded we become. If we don't use the natural skills we have, we lose them.

The thought of leaving your phone at home can induce panic. 'Oh no – I'll be alone in my head.' Fear not! That's why back in the section 'How to use this book' I suggested that you read a milestone before you run. That way you have some good stuff to process while you absorb and enjoy your surroundings.

Racing Tip

Running is an individual sport, but it takes a team of people to assist in the organisation of your event. Many of them are there on a voluntary basis, or their club is receiving finances from the race. If they weren't available, there would be no race. They are being generous with their time. When you get to an aid station or registration table, remind yourself to say thank you or give a thumbs up. Share the good karma.

If you'd really like to demonstrate gratitude towards these volunteers, might I suggest that you don't drop rubbish on the race course. Picking up rubbish is a thankless job that these volunteers have to do after your race. Help them by throwing rubbish in the bins provided or at the distance markers so it can be picked up quickly. Who knows, the Universe/God could be watching. What goes around comes around and maybe someday you will be helping and you'd appreciate the same.

The Seventh Milestone – Law of Attraction

A few years after completing the seven marathons in six days, I entered the Marathon des Sables (the world's toughest race) across the Sahara Desert. This, after all, is more or less what those seven marathons amount to – a 250km run. The conditions, however, were rather different to those that I had encountered in the rain-soaked midlands of Ireland. First of all, you had the intense heat. Up to 42°C some days. Then there was the terrain, a combination of rocky hills and energy-sapping sand. Last but far from least is the fact that you have to run with a heavy pack on your back, containing your food, your cooking equipment and your sleeping gear. The only thing they give you when you get there is water – and you have to carry that on your back as well.

At the beginning, my training regime went very well. I found out about another guy (Paul) in Dublin who was also going to compete, so I got in touch with him and we trained together, round the hills in Howth and in the Wicklow Mountains. At a certain point, we began to run with backpacks, slowly building up the weight in them – aiming for the point where they would weigh as much as those that we would carry in the Sahara. Then, one day, I began to feel pain in my lower ankle. It would ease off when I stopped running, but it never really went away. As the days went by and I continued to clock up the miles, it began to intensify. It got so bad that I finally had to acknowledge that I had a problem, so I went out to the Sports Surgery Clinic in Santry and got an MRI done. When the doctor met me with the results, I knew from the look on his face that the news was bad.

'You've ruptured your Achilles,' he told me. 'All training is going to have to stop.'

I told him what I was training for, and explained that I couldn't stop. There's a long waiting list for the Marathon des Sables. If I gave up my place that year, who knows how long I'd have to wait for another. When I pressed my case, he thought about it and eventually suggested a cortisone injection.

'There's no guarantee that it will be enough to settle it down,' he told me, 'and either way, it won't be enough on its own. You're going to have to modify the way you run.'

He brought me downstairs to the physiotherapist, who began talking me through a way of running which was designed specifically to take the pressure off my Achilles tendon. The moves themselves were relatively straightforward, but adopting them meant overriding the way I had been running since, well, since I learned how to run. It wasn't a question of seeing the moves and then off I go. I had to start small by walking with this particular posture, then slowly, slowly upgrading that walk to a run. I went from being able to carry a heavy pack through a 30km mountainous run to more or less hobbling around my local park.

I remember two old guys sitting on one of the benches in the park, watching me the first time I tried out this new technique. I overheard one of them say to the other 'Looks like that fella's first day out'. But I was determined. I'd been attracted to the Marathon des Sables for years and had visualised finishing the race regularly in my mind.

Sometimes, if you stand back and look at the immensity of the job that lies before you, you can be intimidated into paralysis. So I didn't do that. Instead, I broke it all up into little chunks. The first thing I had to do was to walk comfortably. Next, my aim was to mix a walk and a jog, trying to make a complete circuit of the park. Then, I tried to hold that jogging stance for an entire circuit. And finally, once I had made that new stance instinctive, I could head back out onto the roads again and try to rebuild my fitness. That, at least, was the plan.

I kept my focus squarely on attracting recovery. As I trotted around the park, stopping and starting, I would continually send love and good vibes down to the injured Achilles. And it began to work. I could feel it getting stronger and stronger, to the point where I was almost back to the level of fitness I had before this injury. Then what happened? Because I was protecting my right Achilles so carefully, I had unwittingly been putting too much weight on the left. And then, bang, it went too. We were only months out from the start of the race, and I was back at square one. Off to Santry I went again, where the doctor told me it was time to cash in my insurance and pull out of the race.

'It's very unlikely you're going to make it to the starting line, let alone the finish line.'

I shook my head.

'No,' I said. 'I managed to get the right one working; I can get the other one working too. I know how to do it now.'

So I went back to the park, and I began working on the left just as I had done with the right, first walking, then trotting, then trying to break into a run without compromising that altered running stance. Once again, I broke it down into chunks, chunks which I knew I could do. The truth is that, despite the pain, despite being told that I should give up, backing out never crossed my mind. Never. And the key to that recovery, to that determination lay in my mental preparation.

I constantly visualised the end of the race. Constantly. I had seen loads of footage on YouTube of the French organiser, embracing every single person who crossed the line. He would grab them, hang the medal around them and in good French style, plant a kiss on each finisher's cheek. As I hobbled, then walked, then trotted about the park, I kept picturing that moment, kept recreating it in my head. I would cross the line; I would meet that French guy. I would get my two kisses. It sounds daft, it sounds funny, but that's what I did, and the strength of that image, that visualisation, powered so much of the work I did.

Finishing became central to whom I was; it became part of my being. As I ran, I kept sending down love to those two injured Achilles, and when I wasn't doing that, I was visualising crossing that line in the Sahara and that French guy was rushing to meet me. That process of attraction, that constant visualisation filled me with confidence. I remember in the plane going out, I was in terrific form. At the start of the race, I caught sight of the race organiser and I said to myself: 'Right, I'll see you at the end of this thing for my two kisses.'

But the first day was rough. Really rough. The race organisers surprised everyone with a change of format. Normally, they don't put you on the sand dunes first, because that's the most difficult terrain, and at the beginning, the bags are at their fullest – you eat your burden lighter as the week progresses. Now the world's toughest race had just become even tougher. I really struggled that first day, and at one point – for the very first time – I actually thought that I wasn't going to make it. But when those thoughts, those negative feelings came into my mind,

I tracked back over all the work I had done, all my training, all the pain I had endured, all the sacrifices I had made to get me to this point. I harnessed my energies back to the Law of Attraction, and once again I relied upon my permanent motivator, my key visualisation.

Once I had overcome that moment, everything went perfectly. The second day was easier, the temperature had dropped and I felt stronger than ever. By day three, it felt like a big camping adventure in the Sahara Desert. And, in the end, I got there, I got my medal and my two kisses!

The Law of Attraction

I should not have been able to finish that race. Medically, I had been written off, twice! To make that race happen, I used a combination of all the positive tools I've shared with you so far. In particular, I succeeded by engaging the Law of Attraction, through visualisation and high calibre willpower. The Law of Attraction simply says that you attract into your life whatever you think passionately about. One point to note here is that thinking is not enough. The hidden word in 'attraction' is *action*. To succeed at a higher level, you must take action to back up your thoughts. That is how you get the most from the Law of Attraction.

I used the Law of Attraction to help me finish the Marathon des Sables, but if I had not done all of the preparation, I would have failed. Sitting at home on the couch and willing something to happen will not make it happen. The Law of Attraction works best on things you control. Outcomes you can influence. When other people are leading the agenda, it might not be as straightforward. The Law of Attraction works best when you are making the decisions based on what you can personally influence.

You'll find this law holds true in so many aspects of life. Think about the friends you have. If you are a positive person, chances are you will draw more positive people into your life. We are attracted to people who have the same characteristics as ourselves.

Connected Attraction

All living things are connected. Our DNA differs from those of the higher primates by only 1.75 per cent. And to take it out a little further, did you know that you share 57 per cent of your genetic make-up with a cabbage?

The universe is made up of energy; you are made up of energy. All the time we are either absorbing or releasing energy. If the energy you are giving out is sadness, that will make others feel sad. I'm often moved by something tragic on the news. If you think about it logically, why should we care about some disaster that befalls someone we never met? And yet we do.

We are all connected, and I believe that interconnectedness can be harnessed through the Law of Attraction.

The Language of Attraction

The key thing is to focus on what you want, not on what you don't want. The Law of Attraction does not deal in negatives. Take for example this desire: 'I don't want to get sick.' The focus is on the action word 'sick' or the action of becoming sick, not on the word 'don't'. Therefore, your thoughts become centred on sickness, thereby increasing the chances of you attracting it. It becomes a self-fulfilling fear.

Picture this scenario before a race: you've trained hard and you're confident you can beat your best time. But all you can think about is the bad night's sleep you had and the heavy feeling in your legs. Instead of focusing on what you want to attract, your head is filled with negativity, which might sabotage your chances of reaching your target.

How to Create Attraction

There will always be uncertainties with the Law of Attraction. This is not science. But you have to follow through and play your part. Stay focused on what you want and take action to achieve it. Keep attracting the goal. I've said that in order for this to work you must think about what you want *passionately*. So how do we put these messages out to the universe? We put out these messages using our senses. We do it through visualisation and we do it *kinaesthetically* (by taking action). Clearly, we also do it verbally, but speech isn't the dominant vehicle here. We bring what we desire into our subconscious mind via our conscious mind and from there we send out the signals of attraction. As we continue to passionately visualise this desire, we subconsciously manifest all elements of it in our everyday lives.

To put it another way, whatever we want is on our minds a lot of the time. We emit signals and begin to gravitate towards anything related to our desire, as if our frequency has been met and matched by our desire. The frequency then draws us towards the goal. But you need to take action once you feel the vibe of the frequency. It will show itself. There will be clues, and the more often you use the Law of Attraction, the better you will become at noticing those clues. They will prompt you to take action to bring your goal/desire to fruition.

Daily Attraction

We engage the Law of Attraction every day of our lives, mostly unawares. Our beliefs and values play a role in what we attract. If you're a working mother with two young children, your priorities will be influenced by those beliefs and values. You'll be focused on creating a safe, happy environment for your children; you'll be taken up with trying to balance a career with the need to spend as much time with them as possible. This is what you passionately want; this is what you draw towards yourself. As before of course, it won't happen without stepping up and taking action.

You'll notice too an increasing awareness of whatever it is you passionately desire. For example, you might be interested in buying a certain kind of car. Suddenly, you begin to see these cars everywhere. Prior to that, you never noticed them. Why? Because your subconscious mind understands the passion and desire you have for this item and is sending out the frequency. The more we focus on the goal – having the product and enjoying it – the more we start filling in the means, first subconsciously but eventually through action.

Taking Action

There's a curious phenomenon I've come across again and again with my coaching clients. In the first session, as he or she talks through a particular issue, we'll discover something; we'll stumble on a particular insight. Simply by talking through an issue, the client will become aware of something they didn't really acknowledge before. It will be an awareness, a little piece of self-knowledge that's been hiding in plain sight. Then, when they come back in for the second session, they'll say…

'Eoin! You'll never believe what happened to me after I left your office last week…'

Now, as a result of that heightened awareness, it's as if the blinkers have fallen away and the clues start to reveal themselves. I had one client who was looking for a new job, but consistently failed at the last hurdle. Four times she had made it to the final two, but each time had been pipped at the post. Understandably, this experience was sapping her confidence.

'What's wrong with me?' she asked. 'Why am I not sealing the deal?'

We discussed the situation in detail, working through her preparation and the interviews themselves, forensically analysing the process to try to figure out what was happening. What I began to see – what she began to see – was this: while her competence and focus and determination were second to none, what was absent in any of the interviews she had done was a human side. She wasn't displaying any real warmth. I suggested that she allow her personality to come to the fore in the next interview. Smile. Make conversation. Be pleasant. She was resistant at first.

'I could have done any of those jobs better than anyone else. Why do I need to be touchy feely all of a sudden?'

The truth of course is that we're not machines; we all need to work to connect with each other. If you're hiring someone for a job, yes, you want to know that they can do it, but you also require them to be easy to deal with, to be pleasant, to contribute positively to the lives of those around them. Anyway, that night, she was in the supermarket, thinking over what we had talked about in the session. At the checkout, she did something she had never really done before. She smiled at the person behind the cash register and said hello, and had a conversation. As she left, she realised that she was smiling, that she felt lighter as a result of that brief, inconsequential exchange. Oh my God, she thought, this works!

So she tweaked her interview style, allowing more of her personality to come through. Yes, she was still authoritative and focused, but now she was human too. And of course at the next interview, that little adaptation paid off and she got the job.

Breaking the Cycle of Negativity

The things we are attracted to reveal a lot about us and the story of our lives. Nobody was born negative. If you're going through a negative phase, you're probably sending out a frequency of negativity.

Become aware of your frame of mind; focus on what you tend to think about. That process – becoming aware of how you're thinking and what you're thinking of – is the first step towards making the positive changes you need to make. With that awareness comes the responsibility to do something about it.

Then you have to *decide* that you want to change it. If you kind of want to change but are not sure, you are sending our mixed signals. The Law of the Universe can't help you if you are undecided. If something is unacceptable and is not serving you, then you must change. The alternative is to go through further pain and only change when it becomes unbearable. Yes, **you** must change. You cannot change other people, so if the situation is going to improve you must make the first move – even from a position of pain and being wronged. It won't be easy but neither is the current situation. The difference is that seeking change is empowerment. You take control.

I had a client whose life had taken a major downward turn. When he came to me, his former partner had taken out a restraining order against him after he had attacked her new partner. He and his ex-partner had had a child together and, as a result of his actions, he no longer had access to his daughter. This had a devastating impact on him. Now in his thirties, he was back living with his mother, drinking too much and barely able to earn enough to keep himself.

The first time we met, I saw someone who was stuck in victim mode, who saw no connection between his actions and the mess his life had become. He missed his daughter deeply and, believing that there was nothing he could do to save the situation, he was utterly demotivated. The one glimmer was the fact that he was seeking help. He came to me because of an upcoming court appearance, at which he hoped to convince the judge that he should be allowed visitation rights with his daughter.

One of the big negatives against him was the fact that he had fallen back on maintenance payments. He was self-employed, but hadn't been bothering to work. The first thing we had to do was to turn that situation around and get his maintenance payments up to date. His sole focus, the thing that he was passionate about, that was totally in tune with his values, was to get his daughter back. Working backwards from that generated two simple goals. Stop drinking. Start earning.

The other thing he had to get his head round was the possibility that none of this might work. The judge could very easily extend the exclusion order and prevent his access to his daughter for a further three months. In addition to knuckling down, he had to prepare mentally for the possibility of failure, so that if and when it came, he would not spiral backwards into helplessness again. He came to realise through this process that there was no one to blame for the situation but himself. It wasn't his ex-partner's fault that he had attacked her new partner. It wasn't the new partner's fault. It was his. And in losing control of himself and allowing his anger to take over, he had surrendered control of the situation. The only way to get it back was to change. To work hard and to prepare mentally for the challenges ahead.

As it happened, the judge wasn't convinced in that first court appointment. My client walked out of court knowing that he would not see his daughter for at least another three months, which was when the next court date had been set. This was a blow, and a heavy one, but he wasn't knocked off course. He sucked it up. Falling back into old habits would only take him further from his daughter. So he kept going, kept earning and finally, three months after that, the judge lifted the restraining order and gave him weekend visiting rights. He stuck with the plan, and it paid off. The point here is that **he** had to change. If he truly wanted any control back, the only person he could change was himself. And that's what he did.

The Law of Attraction Clues

When you are calibrated to focus on what you want, the clues will appear. I wanted to have my own business from as far back as I can remember. I was always searching for my bright idea; rising up the corporate ladder held little appeal. I spent a lot of time looking around and thinking about what I could do. What could I do that would make me happy and make me self-sufficient. I had lots of ideas, but in the early days, none of them had enough traction; there was nothing I felt passionately about, but I was patient and never doubted that I would eventually find something that suited my beliefs and values.

And it came. I discovered life coaching at the same time as I discovered triathlon. That left me with a decision to make. Do I pursue sport or life coaching? I had a nine to five job at the time, so I realised I couldn't do both at once.

Again, I looked for the clues. I dearly missed the competiveness of sport, so the benefits of triathlon won out. This took me on some goal-setting sporting adventures, the likes of which I'd never experienced before. Seeking and listening to those clues opened up new opportunities for me.

While a member of the triathlon club, I volunteered to be the race organiser for our annual race. Following on from this, I volunteered to become a race referee and technical delegate for Triathlon Ireland. This gave me a wide variety of experience overseeing and signing off other club races. I discovered I had a keen interest in the buzz and skill set surrounding race organisation. So when I was made redundant during the recession, it felt right to begin a sports events business organising races. Becoming self-employed gave me the freedom and time to study to become a coach.

Eoin Ryan – race organiser and peak performance coach. How did all that happen? How did I end up here? The truth is that I was attracting all these things into my life, all these things that I was passionate about and that were in tune with my beliefs and values. When the clues emerged, I took the opportunities. I'm still taking on new challenges and attracting more opportunities each day. I think of it like this: I have my goals and I'm not afraid to stretch and work for them. As you can see the Law of Attraction is very much connected with setting out your goals, something which we'll work on in the final section of the book.

Get the Law of Attraction Working for You

- Focus on what you want – not what you don't want.
- Ask yourself is it in tune with your beliefs and values?
- Do you feel passionate about this? Marking it out of ten, does it score an eight or above?

- Is this a goal that you are willing to work on, make sacrifices for, and adjust over time?
- Don't just mull over whatever it is you want. Ask for it. Stand up and ask for it.
- Check back regularly. Is this still what you want?
- Newton's Third Law of Motion states that for every action there is an equal and opposite reaction. Remember it is not all about receiving. You have to be willing to give back.

I have found too that my gratitude for achieving these wins demonstrates to the Universe/God that I'm ready to advance further. This cycle of attraction, gratitude and giving back all conspire to make you a more positive person. This journey that you're on as you progress through *Outcome Running* is like connecting the dots. Each milestone on its own is very good. Connecting them brings all that positivity together, making your life so much better.

The Law of Attraction applies to the running side of your life too. Figure out what you want to attract when you go running. Is it a fast time, weight loss, peace of mind, fresh air, feeling good, feeling free – or something else? What is your 'why?' It's important to be clear about it. It doesn't matter if you're an experienced runner or a newbie, when you have your 'why', take the time to drill down into it, to really explore it.

For example: I will take up running to lose weight.

1. Why – I want to lose weight to look better.
2. Why – I want to lose 3lbs in time for a friend's wedding.
3. Why – I want to lose weight to feel healthier.

Drilling down rationalises and solidifies why you are committed to doing this. The aim has deepened from just taking up running to losing a specific amount of weight in a period of time and to feeling healthier. That gives you much more powerful and personal motives to succeed.

Outcome Running: Getting Your Thoughts in Order

Using visualisation to help you to achieve a goal can be really effective, especially for runners. When you're out on the road, focus on something you want to achieve and visualise it actually happening. Then repeat. The power of visualisation lies in repetition. By creating the desired reality in your mind, you're creating the conditions in which it can actually come into being.

Watch for Law of Attraction clues in your own life. Observe your own behaviour. What are you drawing into your life? Where are your passions and values leading you? By becoming conscious of these things, you can avoid years of aimless drift. The key to any change lies in taking responsibility for yourself. Recognise the need to change yourself in order to get what you want. Nothing happens by sitting on the couch and willing it to happen. Get up. Get out. Get doing.

Action Steps

1. Focus on what you want, not what you don't want. Then check it by drilling down to at least three 'whys'.

2. Ask the Universe. Watch for clues. Be prepared to be patient and work hard. Receive. Be Grateful. Give back. Repeat again and again. Take responsibility for your own actions. You are the gatekeeper of your mind. You are in charge of your own emotions. No exceptions.

3. Remember it is not all about receiving. You have to be willing to give back.

LAW OF ATTRACTION

Stage 1

What percentage of your thinking is taken up with things you don't want versus things you do want?

Things I don't want _____ % + Things I do want _____ % = 100%

Stage 2

Think of something you would like to attract? _____
Run it through the check list and answer Yes or No

Is this something you really want? _____
Is it in tune with your beliefs and values? _____
Do you feel passionate about this? _____
Are you willing to work on, make sacrifices and adjustments for it? _____
Have you broken it into sub-goals? _____
Have you asked the Universe/ God for it? _____

Outcome question: How much do you **really** want it?
On a scale of 1 to 10 (10 being highest), circle 1   2   3   4   5   6   7   8   9   10

Running Tip

Beware of negative people and of your own negative self-talk. In a running context, should you find yourself listening to someone talking about all their injuries, lack of training, their bad night's sleep, flatulence problem, etc., make a quick exit and go for a warm-up run. These people will sap your energy. If you recognise yourself as a negative self-talker, it is time to change, starting now. Make that change and you'll be more engaging to talk to. Tell people the good news not the bad. You'll attract more positive people. Remember like attracts like. You'll reap what you sow.

Racing Tip

I have a friend who made four failed attempts at a sub-three-hour marathon. Each time, he came up short by less than a minute. Running a sub-three-hour marathon became a monkey on his back. He started to lose hope. He was picking all the known-to-be faster marathons – Berlin, London, Rotterdam – so his wallet was getting lighter with all the travelling expenses. I suggested that in his next attempt he find the sub-three-hour pacer. Tuck in behind the group and stay there. It worked. He finished in 2:59:38.

When you're racing, the best place you can be is behind someone doing the same pace as you. If you've ever watched a cycling race, you'll understand. Much of the logic there is to use someone else's slipstream to conserve energy. Of course, the speeds are a lot slower while running so the benefits are less. However, any free and easy benefit is worth taking. Naturally, this will work even better on a windy day. Let someone else be the windshield. But try not to make it too obvious! Find someone with broad shoulders listening to music. They'll be oblivious to little old you running on their coat-tails.

The Eighth Milestone– Challenge

I was driving in Dublin one morning, looking for a particular recruitment agency. I wanted to change jobs. The meeting I'd arranged was to take place during my working hours, so I was under pressure to get back to the office quickly. Because the numbers on the buildings were very small, I was driving slowly to try and read them from the roadside. A taxi driver driving behind me beeped and I ignored him. Then he beeped again and began overtaking me. I immediately put up my middle finger. He saw it and stopped dead in front of me. That forced me to stop.

He got out of his car. I got out of my car. He walked towards me. I was already walking towards him.

In the middle of morning rush-hour traffic, right beside a crowded bus stop, we were nose-to-nose exchanging pleasantries with one another. Eventually, we both backed down because it could only go one way from there.

Looking back now, it was all very embarrassing and totally unnecessary. On the surface, he was protesting about me slowing down the traffic. I was feeling angry about the poor visibility of the numbers. When he started shouting at me, I didn't care about his view of the traffic and he didn't care about why I was driving so slowly. We were both coming at this from different angles. The one thing we had in common was anger. For both of us, when we were given the platform to be angry (courtesy of my middle finger), we both gladly took the opportunity to vent it. Beneath the surface, we had other things/

thoughts going on. For me, it was the stress of making my meeting and minimising my lateness for work; I can't speak for him.

Think about this example in relation to yourself. Has your behaviour ever been challenged in a way that made a bad situation worse? It might seem an odd question, but I often observe my clients unable to associate their problems with themselves. Yes, they have a role in their problem, but it's not a causal role. They have disassociated themselves from the outcome. They take no blame.

Take gratitude as an example. Who were you thinking of when you read that milestone? Were you thinking of instances when people weren't grateful to you? Or were you truly examining your own gratitude. It is a challenge to look within and take responsibility for ourselves and our behaviours. We are constantly faced with challenges as we travel through our lives. Very often, that challenge comes down to this. How do I react when adversity strikes? In the example above, with the taxi driver, I responded very badly. I allowed my anger to take over. There was a stimulus – the driver beeped at me. I *felt* anger, and my reaction – my effective choice – was to allow that anger to dominate. I could have chosen differently, but I didn't.

Let's see how we can address this challenge. It's easier when you know and understand how to 'catch' yourself before things get out of control. For that, we need to look at how our minds work. We have a conscious mind and a subconscious mind. We're told that we can hold between four and seven thoughts in our conscious minds at any one time. By contrast, our subconscious mind has a huge database of memories.

Conscious Mind in Action

Your conscious mind is responsible for logic and reasoning. When you do maths in your head, you are consciously figuring out the answer.

It is also the 'gatekeeper' or bouncer of the mind. It decides what information to allow into your subconscious mind. It also interprets information. For example, if someone tells you pigs can fly, you can choose to accept that as true or, based on your own information on pigs from your subconscious mind, determine it to be false. You have seen pigs and you know they can't fly. You process the information as it comes to you consciously. Your conscious mind also identifies information using the five senses: what you touch, smell, taste, hear and see.

Conscious Mind

Security Guard of the Subsconscious Mind

Subconscious Mind in Action

Our subconscious mind is a huge memory bank, just like the hard drive of a computer; all information from the past and present is stored there. Quite a lot of it is stored unknown to us. The subconscious mind obeys the conscious mind. So if you agree that pigs can fly, that's how the memory will be stored. The subconscious mind is also in charge of all involuntary actions within the body such as breathing, heartbeat, etc. It also stores our beliefs and values. These beliefs and values are what form us as people. They are deep within our psyche.

When it comes to challenges in stressful circumstances, we tend to react rather than think. When we do this, we engage the subconscious mind and blurt out the quickest, smartest thing we can think of. The alternative is engagement of the conscious mind. Then we can offer a logical and considered response. It only takes a millisecond, but that millisecond can be the difference between two people standing in the street shouting at one another, or not. It is a challenge to hold aggression back and think rationally, but the rewards for you (and the other person) will be much more positive.

The nub of it is this: we have choices. I had a choice to react to my anger and get out of the car, or to just get on with my day. By choosing to get out, I escalated the situation. Had I engaged my conscious mind and ignored the beeping horn, I could have avoided reliving the scenario in my head for the remainder of the day. That was my first challenge. Mission failed. That unpleasant incident stayed in my head long after it had happened. I had a really bad day as a result.

Okay – so it happened. And as a result it was dominating my thoughts. But what if I had decided not to think about it anymore? What if I had let it go and put it down to experience? How good would that feel? There was another challenge to face. Not easy to do but well worth the effort. Thinking about it all the time only pours petrol on the emotions. Let's look at this.

Thoughts Cause Reactions

Our thoughts determine how we feel. That is the basis of what is going on. So when a memory/thought pops into your head, the association comes with it. Think of the best holiday you ever had. Now think of the worst exam you ever did. These examples evoke contrasting emotions. I want you to take each one in turn and feel the feelings that each inspires. In so doing, you will be pulling memories from your subconscious mind. I'll generalise (for the purpose of this example) and say: holidays = good memories; exams = bad memories. That's how those examples are stored/categorised in our mind. When we recall them consciously, we feel good about holidays and bad about exams. The feelings are linked to the memory.

This is how we recall a memory from the subconscious mind to the conscious mind. A stimulus to remember is triggered in the subconscious. Once retrieved, the memory mixed with the emotion is passed back to the conscious mind leading in many cases to reaction. The consequences of that process, of allowing emotion and reaction to take control, must be dealt with afterwards by the conscious mind. It is the drama that the conscious mind has to deal with post-reaction.

But what if you considered the consequences first? Immediately after the stimulus. What if, in that millisecond after the stimulus, as your emotions began to charge forward, you halted that subconscious urge and let your conscious mind step up instead? In the example of my row with the taxi driver, I bypassed my conscious mind. I reacted subconsciously to the situation. Had I engaged my conscious mind to recall that giving someone 'the finger' generally causes anger, I might instead have just winked and smiled.

Any memory is a spiral, and it brings back whatever emotions, positive or negative, you gave to that thought. Notice how I say *you* gave. Nobody else creates them; they exist in the past tense, in your mind. They are yours; you did this. Once you become aware of how thoughts and the emotions connected to them are formed and stored, you become empowered. The challenge is to 'catch' the reaction at source when presented with a stimulus. We do this via the conscious mind, taking that millisecond to think through where this might lead. Now that you know this, the challenge begins to engage it.

Keeping it positive at a conscious level oils the cogs towards achieving your ambitions

Eoin Ryan – Life Coach

Everything we do in the present affects our future. If we want to have happy thought loops dominating our memories, we need to start at source with being conscious. Rather than getting pulled into an argument, for example, examine the other options. Changing the way you think will change the way you feel. When the thought or stimulus appears, use the millisecond to consider how you wish to react. Based on how you decide to react, an emotion will follow. You are making choices now which will determine how you remember this in the future. Then, when you play the memories in your mind, they will make you feel good rather than bad.

In summary, the challenge is to become conscious of what is happening when it is happening and make your decisions about what reaction is appropriate. Doing that could make your life a lot lighter and give you an amazing sense of awareness. This little tool can be the key to breaking the habits of a lifetime. Making it work for you will take patience and practice. And as for dealing with bad choices? That's your manual for learning from experience. Life is all about learning and experimenting. Now that you have the tools to do both – do you accept the challenge?

My Positive Marathon

My fastest marathon was 3hr 29min. I cracked ribs while water-skiing weeks before the race, then two weeks out, I pulled my hamstring when running. The original plan was to aim for sub-three hours but that was out of the question now. I decided to try for sub-three and a half hours. Even that wasn't guaranteed, considering my various injuries, so I decided to refocus and rather than distract myself with the negatives, my challenge was to concentrate exclusively on positives. I built a huge ring of positivity around this challenge. I constantly reminded myself I could do it, that I was strong, that I was running well, that I was blessed to be there and that I was going to finish inside my target.

That whole process of building up my reserves of positivity is how the Runner's Rhyme evolved. I completed the race 30 seconds ahead of schedule. It was all down to self-belief, positive self-talk and – when it got tough at the end –willpower. I could really feel the 3hr 30min pacers breathing down my neck close to the finish line. Under the circumstances, that was a big challenge completed.

I met the challenge with a positive mindset. I doubt if I would have succeeded without it. Maybe it sounds simplistic but it works. And it works not just for running; it works in all aspects of your life. The challenge is to 'catch' those negative thoughts in that millisecond of

CHALLENGE

Stage 1

Has your behaviour ever been challenged in a way that made a bad situation worse?
Yes / No

Go back to that moment and write down what you would consciously do/say to create a better outcome? _____

Stage 2

Tick the box when you succeed in engaging your conscious mind (taking that millisecond) for a better outcome in your next interaction with the following:

Family	Partner	Friends	Workmates	Strangers

Outcome question: How did it feel to change the outcome by engaging the conscious mind for each? Write a small paragraph to describe how it changed the outcome _____ conscious thought and replace them with something that gives you energy rather than depleting it.

Outcome Running: Getting Your Thoughts in Order

It is a great gift to be able to go for a run, even though it might feel like a challenge sometimes due to weather, energy levels and general wellbeing. I've never met anyone who regretted going for a run. But I have met people who have regretted their preparation before a run. Most of us don't go running on the spur of the moment. Unlike Forrest Gump, we won't dash off our porch and criss-cross America. Generally, it tends to be planned. For some it is a reward, for others it is necessary. Whatever your motive, you will enjoy it more if you are prepared both mentally and physically. Mental preparation could include reading a milestone. Physically, we'll discuss this further in the Running Tip and Racing Tip.

Action Steps

1. Associate the milestones in this book with yourself. Use the words 'I' and 'my' when talking.

2. Practise engaging the conscious mind before you get caught up in the emotions of a memory or new stimulus. Use that precious millisecond to your advantage.

3. In the gap between stimulus and reaction, there is always a choice. Don't let your emotions dictate that choice. Slow the moment down. Make that choice with your conscious mind.

Running Tip

I recommend that you don't run when you are hungry, thirsty, tired or sick. Before you run, always make sure you have enough nutrition and hydration in your body. Good food, not junk. I recommend filling a water bottle everyday and drinking from it. That way you know how much you have drunk before your run. It is easy to lose count of paper cups. Lighter-coloured urine generally means you are hydrated.

If you run when you are tired, it can set you up badly for the rest of the day. Remember, you're trying to achieve greater positivity through your hobby, not the opposite. Running on empty will increase fatigue. If you're exhausted, skip the run. Make a point of going to bed early knowing you will have a longer run the following day. Rest days are training days too. Yes, you have to take your rest days to complement your training days. The important word is complement. Most of the world is on a permanent rest day! I hate to admit it, but the older I get the more important it is for me to follow through on this. Enjoy the rest days. But don't make them your specialty.

Racing Tip

I can't tell you what's best to eat and drink before a race as it's very subjective. I've learned over the years what works best for me. You will discover what's best for you through trial and error and picking up information. Here is one of my funnier rookie marathon errors. At the expo before my first marathon, I heard someone talking about carbo-loading. This, I would later learn, is something that athletes do in the weeks leading up to a race. It's all about building up and burning off your stores of glycogen (stored carbohydrates). It can't be done overnight.

I didn't know that, however, so I went to the Chinese takeaway and bought three tubs of rice to eat during the night. I set the alarm every two hours to get up and shovel in as much rice as I could manage. Not alone was I wasting sleeping time but I was also wasting energy trying to digest carbohydrates which were never going to stay in my body. Plus rice from a takeaway? Seriously?

You don't need to do anything radical or over the top on race day when it comes to food. Be sensible. Work out a plan and stick to it. The more in control you are before a race, the greater your capacity to relax and give it your best.

The Ninth Milestone– Flexibility

Many of my clients find themselves stuck. They have convinced themselves they have no options. They have become so focused on the problem that they can't think laterally. That's where external help can be beneficial. Coaching opens up your thinking and allows you to safely explore new territory that you might not have considered before. Or you can take the initiative to find or create new options for yourself. The more options you identify in life, the greater your chance of being successful. Are you willing to seek those options or do you remain 'stuck'? Adopting a flexible mindset automatically opens you to be solution driven.

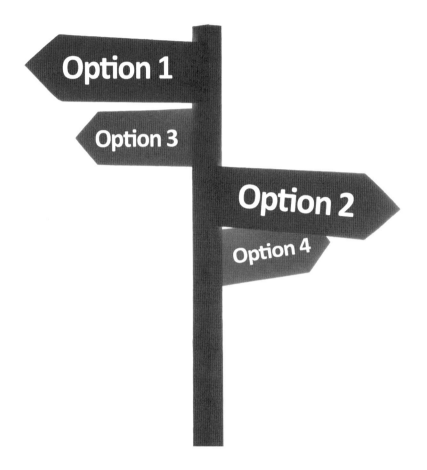

Flexible Thinking

Being flexible is really useful in changing how we see the world. When I ran those seven marathons in six days, I made sure to keep my thought processes flexible. I never thought of the challenge in its totality. As far as I was concerned, it wasn't seven marathons in six days. Instead, I thought of it as running six days in a row. Still the same amount of running, but it sounded easier. And on each day, I broke each 'run' down into segments, from one pit stop to the next.

As the days rolled on and I became more fatigued, I broke it down further – by locks (I was running along the towpath of a canal). On the last day, I was running from tree to tree. Each time I reached any of these positions I congratulated myself and reminded myself how well I was doing. I basically towed myself around the course from one point to the next. Every time I finished one section I was that bit closer to my goal.

If, when you race, you tell yourself, 'I'll never beat my personal best time', you won't. No way. Change your focus and try new methods. Every training session you do should have a specific goal. For example: I need to increase my distance or do some strength work. This is a mini-target that's part of your bigger goal. Training plans, like business plans, are a useful tool but they don't always serve your needs when circumstances change. Flexibility is key to achieving your goal. This rings true especially if you are trying something for the first time.

Say you are training for the marathon or your company is launching a new product. Rarely do things go perfectly from start to finish, so it is important to be flexible rather than robotic in your approach. Most of us are not professional athletes, so we have to be flexible when it comes to training. Work, family and other commitments have to be factored in. Being flexible is about making your strengths work for you in the best possible way.

Life Skills and Flexibility

One word I heard a lot when growing up was 'improvise'. As a family we made the most of our resources. We had spare rooms in our house, and so did bed and breakfast. We had a few acres around the house, so we raised cattle. As a result, with beef in the freezer, we did evening meals for the guests. On the bank holiday weekends when we were busy, my sister and I would often sleep in the TV room so that our beds could be used for guests. We were given the choice and we were cool with it. That was back in the 1980s when Ireland was suffering through a long drawn-out recession. I remembered that flexibility when I was made redundant after the financial crisis of 2008. At the time, I had a substantial mortgage, and I was starting up a sports event business. There were no guarantees of success. In fact, as you've already read, my signature event, Eireman, was a failure.

I could easily have lost my house in the aftermath of that disaster, but I decided to take in two tenants. I slept in an improvised downstairs room for three years to make sure I maintained mortgage payments while I re-established the business. I played the hand I was dealt and adopted a flexible approach. If you find yourself in a sticky situation, with more outgoings than incomings, take a good hard look at your lifestyle. Ask yourself if there are sacrifices you can make, if there's a way of thinking that might open up new possibilities. Be brave. Fresh options are nearly always available to you.

Flexibility and Language

We live in a world of rigid should, would and could – often closely followed by a conditional word.

I should be a teacher *but*…

I would be good at that *if*…

I could be practising *only for*…

Ironically, it is the conditional word (but, if, only for, etc.) that causes the problem. The conditional word is the restrictor. Following that conditional word, a decision/choice is made that determines the outcome. A lot of the time, when people are presented with new challenges that they haven't experienced before, fear kicks in. Those few milliseconds of thought trigger either 'avoidance' or 'curiosity'. Triggering 'avoidance' is very often triggering a fear of failure.

Imagine if we could be more flexible and trigger 'curiosity' rather than 'avoidance' for the majority of occasions? This is something that comes with having a flexible mind and not limiting ourselves to living a life based on fear and withdrawal. It takes time and practice to adopt a flexible mindset. But it's not impossible. As we grow older, we can become set in our ways. Our beliefs about our limitations can prevent us from experiencing new things, from finding new ways to solve problems.

There was once a general belief that it was impossible to break the four-minute mile. Roger Bannister disproved that in 1954. It was considered impossible to climb Mount Everest until Edmund Hillary scaled it in 1953. It seems as though the 1950s was a golden era for curious people. The truth of course is that the likes of Bannister and Hillary weren't the first to try for these 'impossible' goals. There were many who went before them, whose failed attempts were used by those who eventually succeeded to shape that success. I imagine without the failures of others, those guys would not have learned how to better approach the task.

We need curious people so we can help make the world a better place. These are the people who are going to find cures for the major diseases, who will discover cleaner energy sources, who know that failure is feedback and are willing to fail so they can do better next time.

If you're presented with a new experience and find yourself saying the words 'shoulda, woulda and coulda' followed by a condition, stop. Ask yourself: What am I avoiding here? Question your thoughts and words with a flexible mind. Then weigh up the consequences. Am I cool with avoiding this or will I regret it later?

Flexibility is Fun

Back in 2005, I received a letter posted to my workplace inviting me to a University Philosophical Society lecture at Trinity College, where Archbishop Desmond Tutu and Beyoncé would be speaking. This was an exclusive, black-tie event. Now, I never went to Trinity College and I didn't study philosophy. I was immediately suspicious but also curious. I put on a tuxedo and caught the 51B bus into the city. I remember walking around a corner in Trinity and seeing the red carpet lined with photographers. The first person I recognised was politician John Hume, one of the architects of the Northern Ireland peace process. Whatever doubts I had before about this ticket really came home to roost now. There was just no way that it had been intended for me. I paused. I had that moment of uncertainty. There, before me, was the choice: 'avoidance' or 'curiosity'. Do I bow out or do I proceed?

I proceeded. This was going to be an experience I didn't want to miss. I walked up the red carpet. I could see the photographers looking at me quizzically and wondering who I was. One guy took a photo of me just in case. I got to the check-in area and stood behind Mr Hume in the queue. When the guy took my invitation, I could see a confused look on his face. I offered an explanation.

'I don't think I'm the guy you are expecting,' I said. 'I have ID to prove I am Eoin Ryan but I may not be the Eoin Ryan this was intended for.'

The penny dropped.

'No, you're not Eoin Ryan, Dublin South-East TD.'

Indeed I wasn't. So I asked him if I could avail of the invitation regardless, especially since the other Eoin was hardly likely to show up since I had his invitation. He left me to speak to a supervisor. I had one tense minute of waiting before he came back.

'You are very welcome, Mr Ryan,' he said.

I was directed into a room filled with politicians and VIPs. Someone handed me a glass of champagne. I began scanning the room looking for someone to hang out with before the speeches began. As I turned around, I bumped into someone, and when I looked down to say sorry, I saw that that someone was Archbishop Desmond Tutu. We chatted for a good five minutes. It was a great night, an amazing experience. Had I taken the view that 'I should avoid this, I don't belong here', I would have missed out. Instead, I was curious. I wanted to see where it would take me. I didn't worry about being ignored by photographers on the red carpet or fear of rejection at the check-in desk. We only live once – as far as I know. Take the limiters off, be flexible and see where it takes you.

Outcome Running: Getting Your Thoughts in Order

Remember to approach all the situations you face in life with a flexible mindset. You may have a plan, you may have a goal into which you've put loads of time and energy, but sometimes you have to bend in order not to break. Stay focused and realistic, and if you have to amend your goal, don't be afraid to do it.

Running is a brilliant barometer of how well we keep a positive mindset under pressure. What you do when running in a race and how you cope with it will mimic how you deal with stress in the world outside running. Pool your resources of strength to stay positive and upbeat. Make a choice to plant that smile back on your face. Spectators will respond better to you wearing a smile and you'll get their admiration and positive vibe back in return.

Do you remember the Brazilian runner Vanderlei Cordeiro de Lima who was denied a probable gold medal in the marathon at the Athens Olympics by the antics of a former Irish priest, Neil Horan? He didn't receive the gold medal despite an appeal, but what he did get was the Pierre de Coubertin medal for sportsmanship. When he entered the stadium for the last lap, he acknowledged and smiled at the spectators rather than bowing his head and feeling sorry for himself.

Action Steps

1. Take responsibility for your own actions. You are the gatekeeper of your mind. You are in charge of your own emotions.
2. Flexibility is about creating choices. Looking for choices can generate new experiences for you.
3. Be flexible with your thoughts. Aim to trigger 'curiosity' rather than 'avoidance' in that moment of consideration – unless of course doing so puts you in an unsafe situation.

FLEXIBILITY

Stage 1

What is your biggest regret that you didn't follow through on?

On a scale of 1 to 10 (10 being highest) how much does it still bother you ___ / 10

Stage 2

Become more aware of your options. When faced with a future decision, write down your options and critique them.

option 1 _____ : Pros _____ vs Cons _____

option 2 _____ : Pros _____ vs Cons _____ etc.

Outcome question: Stage 1 and Stage 2 demonstrate the difference between avoidance and curiosity. Try this on a current obstacle and feel confident that you reached the best conclusion based on checking the pros and cons for each option.

Running Tip

Most runners are eager to get out the door and start their run immediately. Many neglect to do any form of warm-up or cool-down afterwards. This is a product of our time-poor lives. You've got 30 minutes to run and you just want to get right to it without the tedium of warm-ups or cool-downs. Running with cold muscles could lead to injury. You need to warm up to get the blood flowing, to make your muscles supple, especially if you're doing speed work.

I suggest a five-minute light jog and then some stretching before you start your run properly. And when you finish, do a five-minute cool-down jog, followed by stretching. Factor this into all your training so it becomes a habit. An investment of 10 minutes in each session can save you an hour on the physiotherapist's table.

Racing Tip

Many people wonder how to prepare in the lead-up to a race. This again is subjective. Developing your own routine that fits into your lifestyle would be best. However, the one big overriding tip that I give is to arrive and start a race relaxed. I've run my best races when I wasn't expecting to do so well. Why? Simply because I wasn't wound up about it. I was chilled. Using the content in the 10 milestones will help you to relax. Find the bits that work best for you.

A few more preparation tips include running the race course in advance. Then you know exactly what to expect. Get your running gear ready the night before so you are not looking in the laundry basket for your lucky shorts. Stay off your feet for the last two days to conserve energy. And plan your journey in advance so you know how to get there in good time.

The Tenth Milestone–
Strength

Strength works for both body and mind. To be at the top of your game a mix of both is desirable. Have you ever gone on a run when your head just wasn't in it? Even after you dragged on your shoes, left your house and got the first kilometre under your belt, you still couldn't get into the zone. It's always easy at this point to give up and go home. But you don't. You don't give in. You keep at it and, eventually, you start to enjoy it. Eventually, you're cruising.

From my own experience, it happens now and again that I have to push myself to go for a run. But I always stick with it and don't give up even when I'm not in the mood. I know my mood will eventually change when I'm out running. I believe that it is important to push ourselves, even when we are not 100 per cent up for it, provided we are not sick, exhausted, hungry or thirsty. This builds up mental strength that can serve us well in life.

It takes both mental and physical strength to push towards the line when you are fatigued. You might be in a race and you've been alongside the same person for ages, so that it's become a race between the two of you. You want to win; they want to win. You compete all the way to the line. Sometimes you'll clinch it and sometimes you may not. Winning can be glorious because you competed and found the extra bit of energy you thought wasn't there.

In both of these examples, in order to keep going, you engage your mental strength. These are simple and effective examples of how to build mental toughness. The more you call on mental strength and use it the stronger it will become.

Super Strength

Did you ever hear of people finding superhuman strength to lift a car or a rock off someone to save their lives? In a flash they do something that is beyond what is normally considered humanly possible. It is known as 'hysterical strength'; anyone of us can call on this resource, mainly in life-or-death situations.

Most of us, thankfully, will never have to summon this resource. But what it tells us is that the body is stronger than we might imagine and there are reserves of strength we can tap into when called upon. A lot of this relates to 'fight or flight'. We are programmed to retain some level of energy from the days of the caveman in case a sabre-toothed tiger attacks. So, considering the threat of a tiger attack is minimal nowadays, let's examine where we might now use this energy. Strength is not just confined to physicality. Mental toughness grows the more it is used, just as the fibres in your muscles become stronger the more you work out. Mental toughness needs to be exercised regularly to keep it sharp.

Science Class

One of the core benefits of running is that it releases the two chemicals dopamine and serotonin in the body. These chemicals make you feel good. Dopamine acts mostly in the midbrain. It is a stress regulator for the body. It differs from endorphins in that along with operating the pleasure buttons in our body it also helps with coordination and heart rate. Endorphins are more associated with blocking pain and working the pleasure buttons. Parkinson's disease is associated with the lack of dopamine.

Serotonin is also made in the brain and can directly affect it. People who suffer from depression have lower levels of serotonin; people with low serotonin levels are often prescribed antidepressants to help raise their mood. Illegal drugs such as LSD can dramatically increase your serotonin levels and cause hallucinations. Serotonin has a bodily function as well; about 80 per cent of serotonin ends up in your gut, where it regulates intestinal movements.

So why is this important? As we get older, we produce less dopamine and serotonin. It has been found that dopamine drops on average by

6 per cent every decade. But interestingly, it declines at the higher rate of 11 per cent per decade for the under 40s, before then slowing down. What it does tell us is that much later in life we find it harder to get natural kicks from our bodies. There isn't a lot you can do about that, apart from going on a wild, illegal drugs binge in your twilight years which, of course, I don't recommend! The alternative is to start running and get your kicks naturally to keep the body's pleasure factory working. We will all have setbacks in our lives. With fuller tanks of dopamine and serotonin, we are better equipped to face them head on.

Primary Negative Emotions

Fear, anger, doubt, guilt, resentment and worry are the primary negative emotions that generally knock us back. No matter what stage we are on our journey in life, these guys will always be present. It's important to acknowledge that. However, the more time you give to the negative emotions, the more space they will take up in your mind. You will reap what you have sown. It takes strength to overcome your fears, and it takes time. Any one of the primary negative emotions can build up from time to time in your life. The good news is that anything you learn can be unlearned.

Let's look at fear in isolation. How you become afraid of something depends on your experience of it. At very young age (0 to 7), the experience of a trusted person, such as a parent, and how they reacted to this experience could have influenced you. Allow me to explain. Up to the age of seven, we don't fully engage our conscious minds. We believe what we are told and look up to and copy the people we trust. We don't have the life experience to decide what is right or wrong, true or false. Therefore, if we see a parent reacting fearfully to a situation, we tend to associate that same situation with fear. Fear becomes associated with the experience and the memory is stored in our subconscious mind. Many of our fears are therefore not our own. They are observed experiences. Maybe it's time to question the origin of your fears rather than accepting that they have always been there. Are other people's fears holding you back from new and exciting experiences? So much of what we worry about is in the past, and there is nothing we can do to change the past. What you can do is change how you think and react and worry about it. My quick-fire suggestion is to take the feedback/ learnings from the experience and move on. Your valuable time could be put to better use.

We also spend time worrying about the future. We can't predict the future. We can only help to create it. And, of course, if you are constantly drifting between the past and future, you are missing the present. As we established in the Fifth Milestone, the present is the place to be. Make it your business to reduce the time you spend worrying.

Anger, doubt, guilt and resentment also shape our character. We have all been visited by these emotions; some of you may be experiencing them right now. There is no benefit to judging them as bad. These things are part of being human. If you are in the midst of these feelings, experience them, then find a positive intention from it (more on this shortly). It takes strength of character to face up to your negative emotions. We get stuck in our reality, thinking that it is the only reality. But reality is changing all the time. Something else crops up that soaks up our attention. The information contained in this book will help so that when challenges arise, you are better equipped to manage them at a more controllable level.

Building a Wall of Positivity

If you are facing a particular challenge, the mental prep begins long before the challenge itself. Take a race for example. Your visualisations should start weeks beforehand. You have your target, you know what time you want to beat, or who you want to beat. Begin by creating the experience of yourself running tall and confident and strong during that race. Don't just visualise it. Feel it. Smell the smells, see the sights, hear the sounds. Picture the people cheering you on, feel their hands when they high-five you. What you're trying to do is condition your brain for success. When it encounters the real challenge out on the road, it will all seem familiar – this will be something that you have succeeded at before.

Pump in the positivity. When you go for your training runs, send love to all parts of your body, particularly those that are hurting or tiring. Tell yourself how the race is going to go. Tell yourself how you will succeed. If your aim is to finish, tell yourself that. 'I'm going to run confidently and strongly on the day. Negative things may happen but I'm going to shield myself with positive energy. I'm going to build a wall of positivity around myself.'

When I was aiming for that sub-three and a half hour marathon, I got a bad stitch after taking water at one of the water stations. Generally, when I get a stitch, I tend to slow down or stop to let it pass, but I couldn't afford to do that if I was going to hit my target. So I decided to just run through it. I convinced myself that the stitch was going to go away. I told myself: 'It's going to go. Stitches always go. I'm just going to deal with it in a different way today.' In order to fortify my mind, I used the Runner's Rhyme, which I introduced back in the Fourth Milestone.

'*I look good, I sound good, I feel good.*'

I kept repeating it, over and over again. Yes, it was very uncomfortable, but I was ready for the pain. Preparing for the sacrifice and effort that would be required for this challenge had begun weeks before that. My eyes were on the prize. That was a bigger driver than the desire to stop.

Regrouping

The decision to bring more positivity into your life is open to you. It is a logical choice to want to make but it's going to take strength and commitment to bring about the changes. Sometimes it will feel like taking two steps forward and one step back. But any step forward is a step in the right direction. It takes a strong person to say 'I need to make changes' or 'I need help to make changes'. You are admitting that you are not perfect and that you have room for improvement. That might not be easy to digest at first.

Right now, you may be in your comfort zone. There may not be any obvious 'comfort' in your present circumstances, but if you are not making concerted efforts to change, it is the zone you will remain in; comfortable or uncomfortable. The reason you might be stuck is that your brain is working against you! Yes, you read correctly. Your brain, in the head that you are supposed to control, can resist you. Why? The brain loves comfort zones. Simply put, our brains are lazy. Even if life is unbearable in a 'discomfort zone', the brain will still resist change. It likes familiarity, good or bad. So what can we do? Awareness again is key here. The brain is still yours, you control it. You have ownership and therefore responsibility.

Positive Intentions

Your heart might be telling you that things are not right, but your head is dominating. A greater degree of listening to both is important. Allow me to give you an example of how you might listen to both and negotiate a deal for your common good. The bottom line is that you are looking for the positive intention. To find this, you must drill down and see what (if any) are the positive intentions.

When trying to deal with negative emotions, try to trace back to exactly where the emotion came from in the first place. Ask yourself why you identify yourself with it. What was the incident? What was your state of mind at the time? Who were you with? Recreate that situation in your mind, except this time, stand back from it. Critique it, as if you were someone else, watching yourself in the process of developing that negative association. Looking at it in the cold light of day, does the experience justify the baggage you carry as a result of it?

Knowing what you know now, think about what you could have done to dial back that negative emotion. If this was someone else, how would you advise them to approach the situation? How might they dial back the emotion? By looking back at something with an open mind it becomes a little easier to untangle what exactly happened and the processes by which that negative association developed. Now, ask yourself this: 'For how much longer do I want to hold onto this negative emotion?' Does the kind of thinking that generated that negative emotion serve you well anymore? Isn't it time to move on, and ditch that kind of thinking? Isn't it time to dilute the power of that moment and start thinking afresh?

Finding the Positive Intention

I had a client – a senior manager in a financial services company –who came to me because he wanted to change his job. He told me that he hated his job and needed help to find a new opportunity somewhere else. When I hear something like this, I always like to know more. Why did he hate his job? After some drilling down, it turned out that he didn't actually hate his job at all. What had happened was that the company had implemented a new software system, and that this manager and his staff were not getting sufficient training to enable them to use it properly.

Meanwhile, the legacy system had been retired, and now it was really difficult for everyone to do their jobs properly. This was, naturally enough, causing huge levels of stress in his department, and he felt that the company were not looking after him. So it was this, rather than any genuine antipathy for the job itself, that had prompted his wish to leave. The levels of stress and the lack of control had snowballed, generating this sudden need to get out rather than actually tackle the root of the problem itself. By breaking the problem down, he realised that there would be a way of approaching management and securing the necessary training to make the job doable and to end the stress that was wrecking his working environment.

It seems a simple thing, but so many times, the negative emotions just take over and all you want to do is to escape from them. Turning to tackle them head on, to deal with whatever is causing them in the first place may sometimes seem impossible or too much effort. It was all about finding a positive intention, the key thing that had to be done to clear the toxicity of the environment. As it turned out, this client did leave his employer shortly afterwards, but he left only after the problem had been cleared up. Moreover, he left a department that was functioning smoothly, armed with a very positive endorsement and reference from his employer.

Look at the issue like this:

Head		Heart
I hate my job.	→	I don't feel valued.
I don't like these new systems.	→	I'm frightened to make a mistake.
The training was not good.	→	I'm stressed out over this.
I need to highlight this to management.	→	That will put me at ease.

The employee's dominant head space told him that he hated his job. That was the zone he was in, comfortable or not. He could have accepted this as fact, polished up his CV and left. However, the employee also identified how it was affecting him in his heart space (he wanted this to be a success). From this new level of awareness, he was able to drill down and isolate further what lay behind the dissatisfaction with his job. Finding the positive intention even gave him an action plan to be proactive and do something about it.

To get to a new comfort zone he had to engage the management of the company. This was not necessarily an easy thing to do, but by finding the positive intention he was able to shift his position away from hating his job. The same process can be used to breakdown an issue with your running life.

Head		Heart
I'll never do a marathon.	→	I'd really like to achieve this. But it's so long.
I can run 10K at the moment.	→	I enjoyed that and felt great.
I could train up to a half marathon.	→	Then I'd be mega fit and lose weight.
I could walk half and run half.	→	It would be a big adventure.

Find the positive intention. It can make life easier and allow more space for curiosity rather than avoidance.

STRENGTH

Find a positive intention in something that is blocking you or has formed a block within you right now. Drill down as far as you need to go.

Head

Subject _____

Heart

$\updownarrow$

_____
Keep drilling down to get the positive Intention

Stage 2

What percentage of total thought space are you devoting to the primary negative emotions versus positive emotions **now**? Add the date: ___ / ___ / ___

Currently: Primary negative emotions___ % Positive emotions___ % = Total 100%

Outcome question: Pick one of the primary negative emotions and work at reducing its influence on you. When you are satisfied that you have made an impact, fill in the revised percentage below. Keep changing this as you progress to track your positive development.

Work in Progress: Primary negative emotions___ % Positive emotions___ % = Total 100%

Outcome Running: Getting Your Thoughts in Order

This is the final opportunity to get your thoughts in order before we move onto goal setting. Hopefully, by this stage you have managed to redirect your thoughts and actions into a more positive and productive place. With so much going on in our busy lives, it's easy to drift and forget what needs closest attention.

We all have varying degrees of life experience. I doubt anyone has got to this point in their lives without hitting a few bumps along the way. As it is impossible to quantify positivity for everyone I'll leave you with this question: What can you leverage from this book today that will make your life a more positive experience for you and those around you?

And please remember that nobody is the finished article. Everyone has 'stuff' going on no matter how perfect their lives might seem. Focus your energies within. Your time will come. And when it does – you'll be ready.

Action Steps

1. When you start something that you are really passionate about and in tune with your beliefs and values, keep going. You have the strength of mind or body to see it through. If you stop without making a sincere effort, you have fallen back into a comfort zone.

2. Never be too proud or stubborn to ask for help.

3. Find the positive intention in a setback first before you come to a conclusion and pin a lasting label of 'bad experience' on it.

Running Tip

If and when you start to feel fatigued, try this game to keep yourself focused. Pick a stationary object at least 100–200 metres in front of you. Let's say a signpost. Imagine that this is an important destination point for you. All your focus settles on getting to this signpost and nothing else. Even when you look away from it, you are still thinking of that signpost. When you reach the signpost, congratulate yourself. Say 'well done', 'nice one' – whatever works. But make sure you acknowledge it and give yourself credit. Now pick a new object 100m ahead. Repeat this process until you have arrived at your target.

Racing Tip

Sometimes the weather can have a big influence on your race, and in particular on how you dress for it, especially on those days when it looks like it might rain. It can be difficult to decide what to wear to stay warm and dry. I don't like to run with extra clothes unless it's absolutely necessary. If the extra clothes get wet, it's an extra few grams to carry around the course. But neither do I like to be wet or cold before a race.

My tip is to wear a bin bag. Yes – you read that correctly, wear a bin bag. Get a good-quality bin bag; ideally maximum strength and with a bit of length. Cut a hole for your head at the top and two holes in the sides for your arms. Effectively, you're making a poncho. That way you can stay warm and dry up to the start of the race. Unlike an expensive jacket which you won't want to throw away, the bin bag is disposable. Just make sure you put it in a bin before the race.

Goal Setting on Your Marks

A goal properly set is halfway reached.

Zig Ziglar

Have you ever wondered how you got to where you are in life right now? Do you believe it was luck, faith, destiny or coincidence? If you believe that one of those forces was solely responsible for bringing you to this point, then this chapter will be a revelation. For those of you who have set goals before, I want to sharpen and individualise the process for you. For the record, I do believe in faith, destiny and luck. But I don't buy into them in isolation. Back in the Seventh Milestone, I wrote that the Law of Attraction is about focusing on what you want, not on what you don't want. With that in mind, let's return to where you are right now in your life.

Where you are right now is a result of your thoughts or focus from the past. Think of one significant outcome in your life that is affecting you right now – for good or ill – and trace it back to its origin. Take a moment to join the dots on that episode. How long ago was it? What were the key factors that brought you to that point? It would have begun as a moment or thought in your life and from there it grew, feeding on the focus you gave it. Naturally, not all thoughts will become significant, but some will and that is because you nourished and developed them.

Rather than believing that life revolves around chance and destiny – wouldn't it be great if you could take control and put your focus and energies into something you really want? I'm going to show you how.

Goal Setting: On Your Marks

The first important thing to say here is that you need to write down your goals. A study by psychologist Gail Matthews at Dominican University of California found that those who wrote down their goals accomplished a lot more than those who didn't. It stands to reason. Without a written record of your commitment, how can you truly embed your goals, or check back on them, or hold yourself accountable?

Writing your goals down is just a starting point. I can remember the long lists I made for Santa Claus. I didn't get everything on the list (possibly because I asked for everything in the toyshop) but I got some things from the list because it pointed Santa in the right direction. A targeted list will be more beneficial to you than the shotgun approach of asking for all the toys.

Goals are about who *you* are and what *you* want to achieve. I stress the *you* because many goals are borrowed. If your father wants you to become a doctor, that's his goal, not yours. Remember that if it's not something you are really passionate about, then you will falter. The one thing that all goals have in common is that they must challenge you. If a goal doesn't challenge you, then it's no more than a task.

Beliefs and Values

For any goal to take root, for any goal to be truly achievable, it must be congruent with our beliefs and values. Our beliefs come from our home, environment, friends, culture and religion. We don't all share the same beliefs and our beliefs don't tend to shift much. On the other hand, our values can change. Values are an internalised set of standards with which we align ourselves, and which are appropriate to the particular stage of life we're going through.

Because values are so vital to setting goals, it is important to take a snapshot of your values right now. By recording them, you can ensure that the goals you set will be aligned with those values. If our values and our goals are poles apart, we will struggle to succeed. If, for example, you value donating your time to charity but your goal is to dedicate every moment you have to becoming wealthy, that goal will not serve you well.

What are your core values?

Identify three values in each category that you currently hold/have which are the most significant for you now (in the present). That will give you a total of 15. These selected values will then be used later to help you check that your goals are in agreement with your values.

Note: Words can overlap in categories.

Family/ Relationship	Personal Develop	Happiness	Health & Energy	Finance / Wealth
1.	1.	1.	1.	1.
2.	2.	2.	2.	2.
3.	3.	3.	3.	3.
Assertiveness	Achievement	Belonging	Achievement	Accuracy
Belonging	Adventurousness	Challenge	Adventurousness	Carefulness
Cheerfulness	Ambition	Clear-mindedness	Balance	Competitiveness
Commitment	Being the best	Contentment	Calmness	Consistency
Compassion	Challenge	Continue Improve	Challenge	Contribution
Contribution	Community	Contribution	Clear-mindedness	Control
Control	Continue Improve	Courtesy	Continue Improve	Cooperation
Courtesy	Contribution	Curiosity	Contribution	Correctness
Decisiveness	Creativity	Determination	Curiosity	Diligence
Dependability	Determination	Discretion	Determination	Dynamism
Empathy	Diversity	Effectiveness	Discipline	Efficiency
Enthusiasm	Excitement	Enjoyment	Enthusiasm	Expertise
Equality	Exploration	Faith	Focus	Focus
Expressiveness	Fluency	Focus	Fun	Freedom
Fairness	Gratitude	Freedom	Goodness	Generosity
Fidelity	Growth	Fun	Gratitude	Gratitude
Fun	Hard Work	Gratitude	Hard Work	Hard Work
Gratitude	Helping Society	Honesty	Inner Harmony	Independence
Honesty	Independence	Humility	Mastery	Intelligence
Independence	Inner Harmony	Inner Harmony	Positivity	Legacy
Leadership	Inquisitiveness	Intuition	Resourcefulness	Mastery
Love	Leadership	Love	Self-actualization	Order
Loyalty	Making a difference	Mastery	Self-reliance	Preparedness
Openness	Results-oriented	Positivity	Strength	Professionalism
Perfection	Self-actualization	Resourcefulness	Structure	Restraint
Reliability	Service	Self-control	Support	Results-oriented
Security	Success	Simplicity	Thoughtfulness	Security
Selflessness	Thoroughness	Spontaneity	Understanding	Shrewdness
Sensitivity	Understanding	Thankfulness	Vision	Stability
Stability	Uniqueness	Tolerance	Vitality	Strategic
Support	Usefulness	Vitality		Success
Teamwork	Vision			Teamwork
Tolerance				
Unity				

You will need this list of 15 values later in the chapter on 'Goal Setting Go'.

Mindset Motivation (to gain or avoid)

Many of my peak performance clients come to me having failed to reach the goals they had chosen. The motivation eventually dwindled and they never reached their stated goal. The good intentions just fizzled out. I believe everyone is motivated to change but it is important to understand how your motivation buttons are set. Unbeknown to yourself, you might be pressing the wrong ones. Some people are motivated by a positive outcome (to gain) and some are motivated by avoiding negative outcomes (to avoid). It appears to be a very black-and-white distinction. Let me give you two examples.

One of my clients – let's call him Joe – was married with two children. He was the sole bread winner. He worked really hard to secure a promotion at work, not only because it gave him extra status and new interesting responsibilities. It also earned him more money. We all like more money, but Joe's particular need stemmed from a particular motivation. He had bought an expensive home at the height of the housing boom, and after the subsequent housing collapse, he found himself in serious negative equity and worried about making payments. He began to fret about the consequences of losing his home. His motivation is derived from his view of security. He wishes to *avoid* the outcome of losing his home.

Other client – let's call her Mary – is financially successful. She works equally hard in her job. Not alone is it a job that she enjoys doing, she also wants to go on two amazing holidays a year. She wants to change her car regularly and maintain an up-to-date wardrobe. Her motivation comes from her desire to travel and enjoy a great quality of life. Mary wishes to *gain* life experience.

It is important not to judge Joe as a negative person and Mary as a positive person. After all, both are doing very well in their jobs and are financially successful. Their mindset motivators happen to be different when it comes to that particular shared goal of being financially successful. I said earlier that the motivation can be black or white. But people's personalities are far from black and white. There will be some things you are motivated to gain and some you are motivated to avoid enjoy a great quality of life.

Warning: Do you remember in the Seventh Milestone, we talked about asking for what you want – not what you don't want? The Law of Attraction doesn't deal in negatives. Joe could easily make a fundamental mistake here. If he reminds himself of his goal by saying 'I will keep working hard so I don't lose my house', he is constantly living under the shadow of a negative consequence. This is what I call a self-imposed 'language prison'. Even if you are trying to avoid something, it is very important that you reframe that dynamic into a positive intention. He could say 'I will keep working hard so I can enjoy my home'. If he repeats this on a daily basis, his mindset motivation will remain unchanged, but he has rephrased from 'lose to enjoy' and 'house to home'. A small but significant shift.

You read in the Tenth Milestone that finding the positive intention had a net positive impact. So start with the source of your motivation. And if it is to avoid something, reframe it in a positive mantra. You'll be reminded of this when we talk about mission statements. Motivation is present at the start-up phase of goal setting. It is your 'why'. Why am I motivated to change? Let's look at it from a running or fitness perspective.

Person A: I run/exercise because I want to beat my personal best; therefore, I seek to gain a positive outcome.

Person B: I run/exercise because if I don't I might put on too much weight, which will affect my energy levels, breathing and mood. I am avoiding a negative outcome.

The positive intention reframed for Person B : I run/exercise because I will be slimmer, I'll have better energy levels and I'll feel fantastic. Think about your own mindset motivation? What do you want to avoid? What do you want to gain? And avoid the 'language prison' trap. Find the positive intention.

Motivation is a key element in giving you energy towards achieving your goals. However, if your goals and values are in conflict, your motivation will not be sustained.
Eoin Ryan

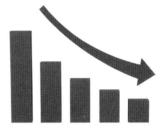

The Vital Importance of Willpower

Motivation is the start-up energy and reserve fuel resource for achieving a goal. Many people will get to the point of action, work on it for a while, and then lose motivation. They feel they have expended so much energy just to get to the 'action' point that they are exhausted.

It's like a plane taking off from a runway. It uses a lot of energy to become airborne. Its momentum takes it higher and higher, but eventually, if it doesn't level off it will use up all of its fuel (the motivation) and that will be that. It will burn out. This is where willpower must kick in to complement or sustain that motivation. Willpower is needed when the initial buzz and excitement of making a change wears off and the temptation towards relapse presents itself. It's that point when you might feel you have done enough. Or maybe when people stop asking 'how you are getting on?'. In weight loss, it's the crossroads where you have lost the first few pounds and feel better but the journey is far from finished. Willpower is the maintenance of your goal.

Willpower, like motivation, is not an endless resource. It needs to be managed. Part of that process lies in reducing the number of opportunities for it to be tested. Saying 'no' to things all day long can be exhausting. You'll use up or deplete the willpower needed to focus on your goal. Then you are relying totally on motivation, which, as we have seen, can run down once the initial enthusiasm wears off. The key point here is that you need to understand the forces that can work with you and against you in achieving a goal. Think of it like this: you need the foundations in a house bedded down first before you hang the chandelier. Otherwise, it may end up an expensive collection of broken glass scattered on the floor.

That is where the ten milestones come into play. Knowing yourself and how your mind operates enables you to better cope with the world around you. So, what can be done to keep the willpower jets firing? It's as simple as this. Eliminate as many situations as possible where your willpower is tested. Be strategic and practical. You want to lose weight? Then remove sweets from the house altogether. When you shop, avoid the sweet aisle and go to the sweet-free checkout.

Without temptation, the opportunities for relapse are reduced, giving your willpower greater scope to embed a new lifestyle. According to a 2010 study in the *European Journal of Social Psychology*, it can take up to 66 days to turn a lifestyle change into a new habit. So turn it into a game. Make it fun. Celebrate your mini-targets along the way. Make a fuss if you hit a milestone. Are you able to high-five yourself? Or better still, high-five an accountability buddy. Another tip for maintaining maximum willpower is to tackle those tough tasks when your energy is at its highest levels. Maybe you are a morning person, in which case get it done in the morning. Or you might peak in the evening. The only way you will find out is by experimenting. A rough rule of thumb is to revert back to the time in the day when you found (or find!) it easier to study for exams.

In summary, motivation and willpower need to be managed. There isn't an endless supply. Part of that process involves celebrating the mini-targets as they arise. That will rekindle your motivation and subsequent willpower. Those mini-targets need to be written into your goal-setting plan. They break your goal into smaller pieces, helping you keep the momentum going. Focusing endlessly on the big picture can leave you demotivated by the enormity of what you're attempting to do. That's why I often use the following strategy.

Motivational Mathematics

When I go for a run, I base it on either time or distance. When I'm doing a job, I base it on time. I like to break things down into fractions rather than focus on the complete distance or job. If I was running 10Km, I'd break it into 2 × 5Km. If I was running for 1 hour, I'd break it into 4 × ¼. Below are examples of charts to use for time and distance. Feel free to create your own.

Time

½ hr: break it into 3 × 1/3 (10 min sections)

1 hr: break it into 4 × ¼ (15 min sections)

2 hrs: break it into 4 × ½ (30 min sections)

3 hrs: break it into 3 × 1/3 (1hr sections)

When it comes to time, I never take it to a fraction smaller than one-quarter. Simply because I find that confusing, and I don't want distract myself.

Distance *(using the km signs)*

5Km: break it into 5 × 1/5 (1km sections)

10Km: break it into 2 × ½ (5Km sections)

Half-marathon: break it into 4 × ¼ (5Km sections), enjoying the last 1.1km

Marathon: break it into 4 × ¼ (10Km sections), enjoying the last 2.2km

I will break the distance into smaller fractions when I have the signs in a race or a satellite watch to guide me. This process does two things. Firstly, it reminds you of how far you've come – so it pushes you on. Secondly, it reminds you of what's left to do – pulling you in. I call it the push on/pull in strategy. Suppose you're running a marathon and you're at the 30km point – getting close to the wall. Based on my distances, that's three-quarters of the way home. So depending on your outlook, you could say to yourself:

- I am three-quarters (¾) of the way there. I'll push on to the finish line.
- I have one-quarter (¼) of the way to go. The finish line will pull me in.

Personally I prefer the pull in strategy. Once I get to halfway – in either a job or a run – I like to visualise the distances declining rather than accumulating. A combination of both can be useful and motivating in any given circumstance. In fact, I'd suggest using 'push on' for the first half and 'pull in' for the final half. There are some who have to be pushed to get started and get the momentum going. Experiment and figure out what works best for you. The push on or pull in strategy gives you momentum towards your goal. As I've said, the big picture can be demotivating. Resistance is triggered because the totality of the challenge is just too hard. The truth, however, is that the only way to eat an elephant is piece by piece. Motivational mathematics helps you to become positively receptive and solution-based.

Get Set for Flow

Before we dive into the process of setting goals, I want to talk a little about something called 'flow'. This is a concept pioneered by a man called Mihaly Csikszentmihalyi, who explains it as follows:

> *The best moments in our lives are not the passive,*
> *receptive, relaxing times… The best moments usually*
> *occur when a person's body or mind is stretched to its*
> *limits in a voluntary effort to accomplish something*
> *difficult and worthwhile.*

Flow: The Psychology of Optimal Experience (1990, p. 3)

Being in flow is commonly associated with sport. The truth, however, is that it can apply to so much more in life. Any journey towards completing a challenging goal will be greatly assisted by a certain amount of flow. Why? Being in a state of flow tells you that you are on track. If you're in flow, you're performing effortlessly, thoughtlessly. You have the sensation that *this feels right*. It is as if the universe is confirming that you're doing the right thing in the right way at the right time. It's an instinctive thing that doesn't really have much to do with the conscious mind.

I can remember my fastest half-marathon very clearly. I did 1 hr 30 mins on a hilly course two months after the Marathon des Sables. I hadn't done much training in between and only really attended the race to hand out leaflets for one of my own races. On the drive down, it occurred to me that I could do a fast time on this course. By the time I arrived, I had bought into the idea of achieving a sub 1:30 finish time.

At the starting line, I can remember joking with the 1:30 pacer saying I was going to 'man mark' him all the way along the course. The truth was that if I had any intention of finishing in that time, I *had* to do that because I hadn't even brought a watch. I started the race well. I felt in control and well-motivated by that 1:30 target. Within minutes of starting, I slipped into flow. But as soon as the first major hill appeared around the 3km mark, I fell back a little and became anxious. The more anxious I became, the more I fell back. When I saw the pacers drifting up the hill in front of me, a little bit of panic started to kick in. I dropped out of flow and worry took over. Then the negative voices started.

At least I knew what to do there. I silenced them with the Runner's Rhyme.

When things flattened out again, I held my own for a few kilometres. I wasn't gaining much ground, but at least I wasn't slipping back. I knew that I needed to find more motivation from somewhere, so I did something I often do in these situations. I made a deal with myself. I decided that I would keep the pacers in view until halfway, then see how I was feeling. The dividend I got from that decision was enough to banish the demons and once again, I slipped back into flow. Once again, I was in control and motivated by that fresh challenge. I relaxed and got on with it. I began enjoying the race again.

At halfway, despite the fact that I hadn't closed the gap much, I felt strong. I knew the worst of the course was behind me. As we progressed to the final kilometres, more people began to drop off the 1:30 pacer group. I don't mind admitting that I got a boost every time I passed one of them out. I was closing on the pacers, but too slowly. I was running out of road in which to catch them. For the last kilometre, I gave everything to tighten the gap. At the start of that kilometre, I estimated that there were about 300 metres between myself and the pacers. I upped the pace but they seemed to match it. Because I didn't have a watch, I was running blind. Were the pacers going to cut it fine to finish just before 1:30 or had they factored in some buffer time?

I gave every last drop on the final 100 metres. I was exhausted but by now I could see the clock, and that stimulated me to take control, embrace the challenge and drive forward. At that point, I knew I could do it, I knew I could make it home in under 1:30. I was in complete flow right up until I passed the timing mat. Then I warmly embraced the first crowd control barrier I could find to help keep me vertical. Job done.

So what happened during that half-marathon? I wasn't in flow the whole time, far from it – I kept slipping in and out of it, which is a common occurrence. When I fell out of flow, I broke my 1 hr 30 mins goal into mini-targets to keep me on track. When I was in flow, I was aligned to the challenge and could maintain peak performance. My belief in my abilities and my actions were in sync. When I was out of flow, I was able to keep going but I could feel the negative voices, the pain, the reasons to pull up building, I could feel myself slowing under their influence. They needed to be shut down, and fast.

Being in a state of flow, or being in the zone as it's often called, is a wonderful experience when you're running. I would describe it as 'poetry in motion'. It's like you've hit cruise control and are effortlessly coursing along. It's important to say that anybody can experience flow. It's not just for fast runners, or experienced runners. New runners who are just trying to get from lamp post to lamp post can experience flow.

Ingredients for Flow

For some of us, flow just occurs naturally and, if so, great! But for those of us for whom it doesn't come quite so easily, I believe with the right ingredients and some diligent internalising, it can be induced. I should say that setting congruent goals is central to this whole process. We'll be going through that a little later on in this section.

The first step is to identify your skills. What are you good at? What are you passionate about? What is it that lights you up with enthusiasm when you contemplate it? You also need to know those aforementioned values. What are the things in life that are really important to you? If you backtrack to a time you last experienced flow, I imagine that you'll see some if not all of these elements were present? You can experience flow when running, when singing, when reading, when painting, writing, speaking...the list is endless. It happens when your talents, passions and values intersect, giving you an experience of effortless, thoughtless joy.

Understanding Flow

You might be wondering if you were ever in flow. Here is how to recap and find your answer.

1. What was your goal at that time?
2. What were your three core values towards achieving your goal back then?
3. What core skills did you use?
4. Why were you passionate to succeed?

That will give you some indication on when and how you felt flow. All these points had to marry together to help you reach flow.

Inducing Flow

Taking some points from understanding flow is a sequence to induce flow, consisting of four steps.

1. Follow the goal-setting plan (coming up).
2. Write down what flow will look and feel like to you when you get it?
3. When in your goal-setting action plan is flow likely to appear?
4. What skills are you going to use or acquire to help get you there?

Joan's Story

I had a client called Joan who was very dedicated to her sport of triathlon. Despite only taking up racing in her mid-thirties she was regularly in the top ten female finishers. In her own words, she was 'all or nothing' when it came to commitment. But even though she was outwardly successful when it came to competition, she couldn't understand why she never experienced flow in a race. For her, it was always push, push, push, from start to finish. She had read about flow and believed that if she could achieve it, she would enjoy racing a lot more and possibly even go faster.

We looked at this and at her personal circumstances. She had a demanding career and two small children. It became apparent, as we dug deeper, that her dedication to training meant that her family life was out of sync. When she trained, she was usually dogged by guilt because she wasn't spending time with her children. She talked about feeling selfish, about feeling like a bad mother. And yet triathlon was really important to her. Not alone did it make her feel good and keep her healthy, it gave her the energy to fulfil all of her other commitments. But when she raced, her mind was frequently taken up with her family and the fact that she had chosen to spend time away from them. It was these conflicting thoughts that messed with her focus and blocked her from entering flow during the race.

That underlying conflict led us to the solution. Achieving harmony at home would be the key to giving her the peace of mind to race freely. We worked on her goals – at home, at work and when she trained – and once they were fixed and planned, I went through the four steps for achieving flow with her. These are the same four steps I use with everyone when we are analysing flow, and the same four steps I recommend you use when you set out to achieve flow in your own life.

1. **Follow the goal-setting plan**. She did. Her goal was to be able to race *and* spend more quality time with her children.

2. **Write down what flow will look and feel like to you when you get it?** For her it meant that she would enjoy her racing more and be open to the possibility of going faster if her focus was just on racing. Flow at home meant she had more time to spend with her children, in particular helping them with their homework and giving them quality downtime in the evenings.

3. **When in your goal-setting action plan is flow likely to appear?** It came quickly. She decided that she would concentrate on shorter distance races, reducing training time (shorter cycles and runs), giving her more time at home. She was able to strike a balance between training and family life.

4. **What skills are you going to use or acquire to help get you there?** She hired me as a peak performance coach to help her acquire the necessary skills. And her partner agreed to help more with the household chores. And if that didn't work out, she decided that she would hire a cleaner once a week.

Is Flow Just a Phase?

I've often heard flow referred to as 'a purple patch'. This notion suggests that it is a temporary phenomenon. If that is your understanding or belief of how flow works, then we need to reframe that for you. If there is one group of people who continually demonstrate that flow can be permanent, it's the All Blacks rugby team. They are statistically the most successful sporting team in human history. In their own words, their success is built 'with the flow, movement, strength, determination, power and speed of Tangaroa'. Tangaroa is the Maori god of the sea. The All Blacks are consistently world class. They can keep flow going right throughout the game, and that has as much to do with culture as with skills. As kids, they are never far from a rugby ball, and that gives them a certain amount of instinct when it comes to the core skills. When those skills are challenged even further by coaching, they are on the road to flow. Harnessing all of that individual flow generates the unstoppable force that the All Blacks have become.

For an example outside the world of sport, look at Oprah Winfrey. She became a household name as host of her own TV show. This programme lasted 25 years and was consistently one of the highest rated shows on television. That is a long time to remain at the top of your game. Was Oprah only hitting flow in patches? I don't think so.

When Will Flow Come?

We live in a fast-moving world where instant gratification has become the norm. The truth, however, is that if you wish to induce flow, you will need to be patient. Things will not always go smoothly in life. We will hit obstacles that can derail us. Half the battle is knowing this, so your expectations are tempered. Overcoming those challenges can be seen as a stepping stone to flow or, depending on how you manage them, an indication that you are already in flow. Flow is not just the end product of achieving your goals. It is the momentum developed while pursuing them. So flow can occur at any stage. When we have it, we need to nurture and maintain it.

How to Maintain Flow

The only way you can maintain flow is to recognise that you have it in the first place. If you don't recognise it, how can you maintain it? Sounds a bit simplistic – and it is! Everyone experiences flow, but not everyone recognises it. Most of us tend to be totally unaware of it or pass it off as a moment or 'patch'. Look back on periods of your life where you were in the zone, when you were performing effortlessly. That was flow.

Flow is the point where the task doesn't seem as difficult anymore. Your skill level has risen to meet the challenge. Flow can occur at any stage along the path towards achieving your goal. It could come early. If this happens, it can give you the false sense that the remaining challenges will be easy, and that could derail you and dilute your motivations.

- Have a clear picture of what flow looks like to you, so you recognise it when you get there.
- If you reach flow, embrace, enjoy and acknowledge it.
- If flow comes too quickly, you need to recalibrate your goal-setting plan. Redrafting the time frames, if necessary, to keep that edge. Think of my 1:30 half-marathon. I was adjusting continually during the race to maintain flow.

- Build from there. See it as a stepping stone reached. Raise the bar if necessary.
- Believe that this flow is long term and is yours to keep.

With the right attitude, calibration and control, together with a great goal-setting system, we can all pursue and achieve flow.

Goal Setting Go

One thing that is certainly going to happen upon setting your goals is change. Change brings unknowns into our lives, and that can be scary. These same changes might also seem a million miles away and unachievable. Fear of change and the long path to change could add legitimacy to an argument against goal setting. But as far as I'm aware, we will only pass this way once, so why not go for it? Henry Ford had a saying: If you always do what you've always done, you'll always get what you've always got.' Be daring. I dare you.

The Running Goal

Naturally, it is up to you what goals you choose, but whatever it is, I'd always recommend including a running target as well. It might be an improvement on your personal best, or the completion of a marathon, or simply finishing a local 5K. The physical benefits that you will realise along the journey towards your running goal are a fitter and healthier you. The mental benefit is achieving something that stretched your resources beyond what you thought you could handle, back when you set the goal. It becomes a beacon of success that you can store in your mental toolbox. One success can lead to further successes. Success then becomes a habit.

Goal Setting: Go

I'm now going to take you through the steps to create a world-class goal-setting plan. Please don't be tempted to skip ahead here. Take your time and work through the system.

Step 1: Passion Reminder

When it comes to choosing goals, it is very important to pick something you are passionate about. If you become stuck, it might be a good idea to reread the Second Milestone on passion. Otherwise, here are a few tips before we begin goal setting to help you refocus your passions: Do you get a tingle of excitement from just thinking about this goal? A little buzz? An increase in your heart rate? Or a sense of knowing that this is right?

Find your area of excellence (based on your skills or talents), the things that you do naturally well. Often they are right under your nose. Ideally, identify a goal that will give you both present and future happiness. For example: I want to cut down on my drinking and get fit. More money and time spent away from the bar creates an opportunity to join a sports club and do more training. You still have the social element without the booze.

Figure out your major purpose in life – your primary goal. Achieving that one goal can often pave the way for all your other goals. For example, I had to make a choice to go back to contract marketing work or become a full-time peak performance coach. I chose to be a full-time coach, and as a result this book was conceived.

Step 2: Selecting Your Goals

First, get a pen and a notepad (that you plan to keep), and a watch to record the time. Allow yourself one hour and a half of quiet time to do this. Ensure there are no distractions. Some of you may actually need a little more time than this to complete the goal-setting process. However, for those of you who work better under the clock, I've included suggested times to follow. The most important point is that you complete everything. Put your phone away or on silent (if it's your stopwatch), get comfortable and begin your goal-setting journey.

We'll begin by segmenting your goal(s) into three categories.

1. Personal development goals (such as writing a book, travelling, doing a course, starting a new hobby, a sporting, a relationship, or contribution goal). Essentially, this is anything that brings you more positivity and helps you develop as a person.
2. Financial goals (such as earning more money, a promotion, setting up a business, investing). A very matter-of-fact category.
3. Things goals (such as a house, car, clothing, tattoo, pet, etc.).

Note: You can of course add an extra category: business goals, for example. Make space on the 'Sun'ary© sheet, if necessary.

Part 1: Categorise Goals

Spend three minutes writing down as many things as you can think of in personal development goals. Repeat for financial goals and things goals in Table 1. (Copy Table 1 into a notebook if/when you do goal setting for the second time.)

Note: I want you to pick things that could happen within the next three years, ideally.

Table 1: Categories of goals

1. Personal Development Goals						

2. Financial Goals						

3. Things Goals						

Total time: 9 mins (3 mins each)

Part 2: Timeframe

Go through all of the goals you wrote and put a timeframe on each one. If you think you will complete a goal in one year, put a 1 in the smaller box beside the goal; 2 for two years; 3 for three years.

Total time: 4 mins

Part 3: Selection

Select your top three Year 1 goals from all three categories. These are the ones you are most passionate about and motivated to achieve. Don't worry if you don't have nine Year 1 goals in total. Work with what you do have.

Total time: 4 mins

Step 3: Proofing Your Goals

If you have set goals before and had mixed results, then you may already have some preconceptions regarding your ability to succeed. This is why proofing your goals is important. It will help to ensure you are close to or at the bullseye. The list you made from Step 2 has to be challenged before we can go any further.

Part 1: 3 × Whys

Again, you'll need a notepad for this. Using the top three Year 1 goals from all three categories you selected in Step 2 (Part 3), write down *why* you are motivated and committed to succeed. You can do this in sentences or bullet points. If using bullet points, copy the structure in Table 2 into your notebook so all the goals are located together for reference.

The first why should be your main reason. The second and third are an opportunity to either drill down from the first why or to put in lesser but valid reasons. Ideally, you should be able to come up with a minimum of three whys to prove to yourself that this is a compelling goal for you.

Table 2: 3 × Whys

First why _____

Second why _____

Third why _____

Mindset motivation (avoid or gain)? _____

Motivational score 1–10: _____

Note: If you find your three whys are coming up short on rationale, move to the next goal. It might be a sign that the goal wasn't as high a priority as you imagined. Come back to it later.

In this exercise, I'm going to allow you to take your time due to the importance. However, if you want to be kept on the clock, the allotted time is as follows.

Total time: 45 mins (or 5 mins per goal)

Part 2: Mindset Motivation

Check back over your 'whys' and decide what they tell you about your mindset motivation. Are you (a) trying to gain a positive outcome or (b) trying to avoid a negative one? Remember, avoiding a negative outcome doesn't mean you're a negative person. What we're trying to do is to match your thoughts with your feelings on why this goal is important to you. Call it as you read it.

Total time: 9 mins (1 min each)

Part 3: Motivational Score

Looking back over what you wrote, score from 1 to 10 on how motivated you are to see these goals through. For example: 1 is very low motivation and 10 is extremely high motivation. Write that in the space beneath your three whys.

Total time: 4 mins

Part 4: Double Check

Now that you have gone into greater depth on your goals, take a second look at the timeframe you originally put against each one in Step 2, Part 2. Make sure you have your best estimate, then proceed to Step 4.

Total time: 2 mins

Step 4: Writing Your Goals on the 'Sun'ary© Sheet

Well done! It takes commitment to stick with it and get all the details down. What's more, it's something very few people ever do. Already you have given yourself an advantage and created a great start on the road to success.

Part 1: 'Sun'ary© Sheet

Next we are going to populate the 'Sun'ary sheet (on the following page). I highly recommend that you download this sheet from my website (**www.eoinryancoaching.com**) click on Books, so you have an A4 copy to work with. I also recommend you print off at least two copies. Use the first one as a draft and then polish it up when you compile the second. You will need this A4 'Sun'ary© sheet later in the process.

Write in your nine (if you have nine) Year 1 goals from Step 2 in the inner circle containing the nine lines titled Year 1 (9 x Goals).

Note: Do not write in the centre circle containing the text 'Your Primary Goal'. Not yet.

Total time: 2 mins

Pause here: Before you write your Year 2 goals in the circle titled 'Year 2 Goals', check if there is a link between your Year 1 and Year 2 goals first (like the business example provided on the 'Sun'ary© sheet). If there are links, copy the business course example and put them beside each other in their respective circles.

Total time: 2 mins

Now write in your Year 3 goals in the circle titled 'Year 3+ Goals' and again look to see if there is a link from Years 1 to 2 to 3. Do not worry if there is not; I don't expect that to happen all the time.

Total time: 2 mins

Linking your goals shows a cause and effect, or link pattern. Completing one goal may lead directly to starting on the next one.

Note: There is an outline of a filled-in 'Sun'ary© sheet in Step 6, if you'd like to take a look.

My Goals 'Sun'ary®

Year 3+ Goals

Year 2 Goals

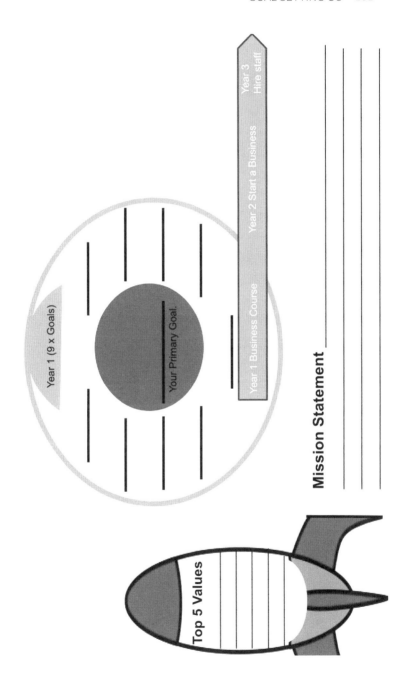

Year 1 (9 x Goals)

Your Primary Goal.

Year 1 Business Course

Year 2 Start a Business

Year 3 Hire staff

Mission Statement

Top 5 Values

Part 2: Primary Goal

Take a good look at what you have written on the 'Sun'ary© sheet. Go back to your Year 1 goals in the inner circle. Is there any one goal that, if completed, will set a platform under or ignite all other goals? Or is there one primary goal higher in importance and motivation than the others? If there is, put it in the centre circle.

Total time: 1 min

Tip: If you are not used to setting goals, it might be a good idea to start with a primary goal that you have the best chance of achieving, or one that you could achieve in the short term, i.e. within a year. That makes success that little bit easier, and gives you momentum for perhaps a more ambitious goal.

Your first draft of the 'Sun'ary© Sheet' may look a mess – particularly if you use the page in the book, and that's fine. As I suggest, later in the process you can download and print the 'Sun'ary© sheet' from

(**www.eoinryancoaching.com**) click on Books.

Part 3: 5 x Values

Go back to the 15 values that you identified earlier in this chapter. Put a circle around the five values that you consider to be the most important to you when it comes to achieving your goals. Once identified, write them on the 'Sun'ary© sheet where it says 'Top 5 Values' (inside the rocket).

Total time: 3 mins

Part 4: Mission Statement

A mission statement is commonly used in companies to keep everyone on the same wavelength. It could be as short and sweet as 'Continuous

Improvement' or more detailed like Facebook's: 'The mission of Facebook social media network is all about the global sharing and connections made possible by the Facebook platform.'

Individuals can also write thought-provoking and motivational mission statements. When you write your mission statement, think of your values. Hone the five you picked earlier down to just two. Now check in with your goals, starting of course with your primary goal. Does it suggest the direction in which you want to take your life? It might. If it doesn't, maybe look for links between the Year1 and Year2 goals. Do they suggest the path? All of the prompts and clues are right there on your 'Sun'ary© sheet. Remember, always write your mission statement in the positive. If you are seeking to avoid a particular scenario, reframe it in the positive. Tell yourself what you want, not what you don't want.

Here are some examples of mission statements from some well-known people:

To serve as a leader, live a balanced life, and apply ethical principles to make a significant difference.

Denise Morrison, CEO of Campbell Soup Company

To have fun in [my] journey through life and learn from [my] mistakes.

Richard Branson, founder of the Virgin Group

To be a teacher. And to be known for inspiring my students to be more than they thought they could be.

Oprah Winfrey, media proprietor and TV personality

It's often a useful exercise to share your mission statement with other people in your life. Remember that the more support you get, the more likely you are to succeed on your mission. Bear in mind too that mission statements are not set in stone. They will vary as you go through different stages in your life.

Total time: 5 min

The 'Sun'ary© Sheet

Keep your completed 'Sun'ary© sheet close at hand. Many of my clients hang it up on the wall or have it displayed on the screens of electronic devices. Pinning it up the wall or have it displayed on the screens of electronic devices. Pinning it up somewhere where you see it often integrates your goals into everyday life and familiarises them for you. It keeps them to the forefront of your mind and allows the Law of Attraction to kick in. If you haven't already guessed, the term 'Sun'ary© sheet is a play on words and imagery. It is essentially a summary/map of your goals renamed 'Sun'ary©. The imagery I use is the sun (if you print it off in colour this will become more noticeable). The sun burns hottest at its core, which fuels the remaining mass of the sun. That is where your primary goal is located. The rocket containing your values will help propel you towards those goals. Yes, we have a bit of a space theme going on here. The Universe is waiting for its instructions from you…

Step 5: Action Plan to Celebrate the Mini-Targets

You have written and proof-checked your goals – good job! Next comes your action plan. You need to have an action plan for each of your goals. I suggest you create an action plan on a computer to suit your own needs. It should contain (at least) these four fundamental headers:

1. Action/ Mini-target
2. Done by whom
3. Date/deadline
4. Result

Goal: - Write a book

Action/ Mini Target	Done by whom	Date/ Deadline	Result
Write the 10 milestones	Eoin	July 31st	Done
Agree the images	Eoin/ sub editor	Aug 12th	Done
Agree the book cover	Eoin/ sub editor	Sept 18th	Pending

This is where you 'chunk it down' into smaller sections. Fill in all of the actions that need to be completed in order to achieve your goals. The more time you spend thinking the plan through, the greater your chance of success. And you can look back at all the mini-targets you have achieved within your goals to show your progress and help keep you motivated. I strongly suggest that you record your first action now or within the next three days. This will help you to really commit to your goals. Remember the positive intention behind writing down the goals involves following through and acting on them. Starting now, write down actions/mini-targets to be completed within the next three days. Do it!

Note: It isn't uncommon not to know your action plan from start to finish. Sometimes you will need to leave gaps. Very often those gaps will fill themselves in as you learn, grow and develop along the journey. Trust that the Law of Attraction will guide you. If your motivation and willpower are strong, you'll find the way.

I've said this before, but it's worth repeating. When you reach those mini-targets, make sure you acknowledge or celebrate them. This will keep your motivation and willpower going. Be mindful that the celebrations don't undo any of your good work!

Step 6: Vision Board and Accountability Buddy

Vision Board

Now that you have your 'Sun'ary© sheet completed, you could take it a step further and attach cut outs from magazines or downloaded pictures showing what you want. The sheet now doubles as a vision

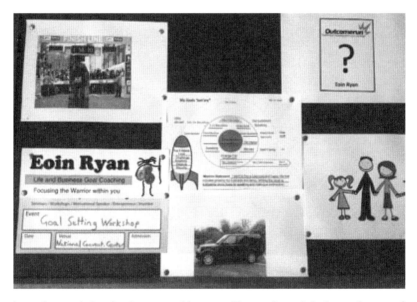

board containing both text and images. Examples might be a picture of a car you'd like to own or a holiday destination you'd like. This works in conjunction with, or as a substitute for, visualisation.

You have kinaesthetically written down your goals and now you are adding a visual touch. Take the new car example – most car salespeople like you to sit in the car so you can see, touch, smell and drive it. They want you to begin associating yourself with ownership of this car. That brings the sales person closer to their goal of making a sale. Making the goal as real as possible helps to test your values and reaffirm that you are willing to make an effort to succeed.

A word of warning. It can happen that if you obsess about something and visualise it constantly, you may become demotivated. Seeing and thinking about it all the time can trick the mind into thinking you already have it. That could slow down or stop your motivation towards achieving the goal. I alluded to this in the Fourth Milestone on feedback. It's vital that you be honest with yourself at all times.

Accountability Buddy

Should you share your 'Sun'ary© sheet with a trusted, positive friend? Absolutely. I use the words 'trusted' and 'positive' for a reason. Some people can project their own insecurities onto you and erode your positivity. Be mindful of who you share your goals with. A locus of positivity will go a long way towards supporting you when the occasional doubts creep in.

Once you have shared you goals with your friend(s), ask them to hold you accountable for the action plan. Better still, share the action plan with them and ask them to check in with you at each deadline to see if the mini-target is complete. You can return the favour for them. This is the best scenario you can have with an accountability buddy. You are now accountable not just to yourself but to others. That tends to sharpen us up more. We never want to look bad in front of others.

I shared some of my big goals, including the Marathon des Sables, the Austrian Ironman, the seven marathons in six days, with everyone, including the media. Plus, I did them all for charity, which made me even more accountable, in my own mind at least.

Step 7: The Checklist

This step is important to keep you honest. When I was younger I used

Goal-setting checklist

Did you pick your 15 values from the list? And narrowed it down to five core ones.
Yes☐No☐

Did you feel passionate/excited/motivated towards achieving those goals?
Yes☐No☐

Have you written your goals down and put a realistic timeframe on them?
Yes☐No☐

Have you drilled down through the 3 × Whys and your motivational mindset?
Yes☐No☐

Did you download the 'Sun'ary© sheet and write goals, values and mission statement on it?
Yes☐No☐

Have you broken each goal into an action plan with mini-targets?
Yes☐No☐

Is the 'Sun'ary© sheet located in a place that is easy for you to regularly see?
Yes☐No☐

Did you add images to your 'Sun'ary© sheet, creating a vision board?
Yes☐No☐

Do you have a trusted and positive person to be your accountability buddy?
Yes☐No☐

Did you complete the checklist?
Yes☐

to read a lot of self-help books but I never did the exercises. Then I'd wonder why nothing was changing for me. Some of you will know what I'm talking about here and where I'm going with this. You need to follow all the steps. If you do, it could be life-changing! Is that worth an hour and a half of your day?

Don't underestimate any of the steps involved in setting out your goals. If you only half do it, if you don't give it your full attention, how can you expect great things to happen? Remember, our lazy brains will resist change. They will keep you in your comfort zone for as long as they can. If you like where you are now and it is serving your needs and wants – good for you! However, should you wish to make changes in your life and take it to another level, you now have the tools.

Common Goal-Setting Blockages

In times past, before I became a coach, I'd sometimes put off the most important jobs on my to-do list because I was afraid I wouldn't get the answer I was hoping for. I can recall during the early days of my sports events company, there was a lot of scaremongering about new rules and regulations coming into force. I listened to all of them, believed them and worried myself silly about them. The sources seemed credible enough but the truth was that they were all just rumours. Because of the fear that they might be true, I avoided finding out the truth.

For example: I would delay bringing my event plan to the local authority just in case they said no, because if they said no, that would be weeks of work down the drain. I felt really vulnerable in those early days because my mortgage was on the line. I was totally relying on this business to succeed. But by stalling on taking action, I gave myself the gift of unnecessary stress. I pondered and procrastinated and often didn't sleep well. Eventually, I would face up to the issue and 70 per cent of the time, I got the answer I was looking for.

Don't make the same mistake. Bite the bullet, grab the nettle. Go for it. Today. Now. Have your mini-targets prepared and go for it! There is nothing to be gained from tying yourself up in a knot. Most requests require either a yes or no answer. That gives you a 50 per cent chance of getting a positive result. If you need a reply or help, simply ask for it. It is pointless to second guess someone, or role play a list of reasons why they might say no. From my own experience, that kind of thing just killed momentum and wrecked my head. Better to know the score so you can continue to focus on your goal. Face up to roadblocks when they appear. The sooner you do this, the sooner you can find a way around or over or through them. The longer you leave it, the bigger they'll get. And remember you'll never be totally ready. The perfect moment never arrives, so take a leap of faith and go for it.

And If I Don't Succeed?

Success is not guaranteed, folks. I have failed – often. I talked earlier about how the first major sports event I organised blew up in my face. The negative PR made it impossible to revive the event the following year. That was *not* my goal. But I learned from it. I now delegate a lot more, plus I have a backup plan in place, so that when disaster strikes, it's not really disaster at all. To put it simply, I started again – only smarter. And now I run a successful business, thanks to that failure. My goal may have been tweaked a little but it was in line with my passions and my values, and despite that very major setback, I was able to stand up, refocus and recommit to that goal.

Goals: The Wrong Way

Goals are future-based personal desires which begin as thoughts. The key word here is 'future'. You don't have them/it yet. Any of the planning you do towards achieving your goal is done in the present. If you have taken the time to go through the seven goal-planning steps, you did it in the present moment (possibly the past now, if completed).

Have you ever heard someone say, 'Well, if I can only get this finished, then I'll be sorted'? This is the chattering mind of someone living in the future and not the present. This is mortgaging present happiness for the promise of future happiness. What if your goal takes you three years to complete? Are you willing to remain in a state of longing for three full years? Focusing on the goal is important but what's equally important is having a balance in your life. If you are miserable for three years, do you honestly think you will enjoy the goal when it is achieved? Will you stick at it? Would it be worth it?

There is a danger of becoming goal-obsessed. Then when you reach that goal, it may not deliver the promised happiness. So you try another one. Same result. And another one... While all this is happening, you are missing out on enjoying life.

Remember, a goal that gives you both present and future happiness is the sweet spot to aim for. Not always possible, but that's the aspiration. I always wanted to be self-employed. When I started my events business, I became an instant workaholic. My goal was to make my business a success, and I worked doggedly on it. I didn't run or do any exercise for months post set-up and clocked up 12-hour days, seven days a week. I put on weight, my energy levels sank. Was I happy? Not at all. I was motivated and busy but not happy. And ultimately my marquee event was a failure. In hindsight, would I have been better off mixing work and fun? Absolutely!

Live in the present and don't become future-obsessed. Strike the balance.

My Positivity is Dipping

Speak to your accountability buddy. Reread a milestone in the book that really resonated with you. Take a break if you have been overdoing it. Or go see a coach. Getting external help is very often the key to maintaining momentum and making sure that your willpower takes over when that initial spurt of motivation wears off.

Action Steps

Follow the system set out here. Take the hour and a half to set your goals. Your future self will thank you.

And Finally

People talk a lot about change but never act on it. Mostly because they don't know how. By reading this book and doing all the exercises you have an opportunity to open up a new level of awareness. That can be both exciting and scary, depending on your motivational mindset for change. Either way you have the foundations to consciously take your life and your running to the next level. The alternative is to continue on with any non-supporting beliefs leading to a predictable (same old, same old) outcome. Remember our old selves will kick back and resist change. You know that now. Expect it to happen. When it does, you'll be ready.

Now is the time to 'grasp the nettle' and bring that change into your life. Believe in the goals you have worked out. Start following your plan and make things happen. You'll never be completely ready, so trust your instincts and go for it.

> *Most people dream big in life. If your dreams are*
> *big, then you must be willing to stretch and grow*
> *to fit into your dreams.*
>
> Eoin Ryan

The same applies to your running. No matter how slow you might think you are at the beginning, you are quicker than everyone sitting on the couch. Over time, with clear goals and a good plan, your running will improve. And so will your life.

I was in what I'd term a 'life concussion' when I stopped being active in my twenties. I had no energy and little positivity. The big change happened when I decided that I had to change. I'd had enough of my stagnated life and the social stereotypes I was conforming to. I returned to what I truly valued which was sport and helping people.

We are at the end of *Outcome Running*. Each time I reread it while editing, it highlighted something new I needed to focus on that day. I would suggest reading a milestone before you go for a run. Give it some thinking time while you are out enjoying yourself. You can dip in and dip out whenever you feel the need for a boost.

> *You can only reliably influence your future by*
> *what you do in the present.*
>
> Eoin Ryan

A reminder when you achieve your success – make sure you celebrate! I'm going to celebrate finishing this book. But it is just the start for me. As you already know, I 'walk my talk' and do all my own stunts. I have clarity in my future goals to help as many people as I can. Please let people know about this book if you found it helpful, inspiring or grounded in a reality that is relatable.

Stay in touch by joining the Warriors Clan newsletter. This will give you information and updates on future events and seminars I run. Go to **www.eoinryancoaching.com** to join this newsletter. It has been my pleasure to guide you through the ten milestones. Expect to see more books, online talks and seminars coming out in the future. Thank you and remember to enjoy your journey.

TRAINING PLANS ONLINE
I have created a 12 week training plan for a beginner 10km, an intermediate 10km and a beginner half marathon.
Go to **www.eoinryancoaching.com** click Books tab, then downloads.

Notes

Notes

Notes